I0490365

ART BOOKS

FROM CRESCENT MOON PUBLISHING

Leonardo da Vinci
by James Pearson

Early Netherlandish Painting
by Rosalind Mutter

Piero della Francesca
by Naomi Haskell

Giovanni Bellini
by Julia Davis

Eric Gill: Nuptials of God
by Anthony Hoyland

Minimal Art and Artists In the 1960s and After
by Laura Garrard

Postwar Art
by George Knighton

Vincent van Gogh: Visionary Landscapes
by Stuart Morris

Max Beckmann
by Stuart Morris

Egon Schiele: Sex and Death in Purple Stockings
by D. Simon Eade

Mark Rothko: The Art of Transcendence
by Julia Davis

Jasper Johns
by L.M. Poole

Brice Marden
by Laura Garrard

Frank Stella: American Abstract Artist
by James Pearson

Dürer

DÜRER

BY HERBERT E. A. FURST

CRESCENT MOON

First published 1910. This edition © 2018.

Printed and bound in the U.S.A.
Set in Book Antiqua 10 on 14pt.
Designed by Radiance Graphics.

British Library Cataloguing in Publication data

ISBN-13 9781861716200 (Pbk)
ISBN-13 9781861717306 (Hbk)

CRESCENT MOON PUBLISHING
P.O. Box 1312, Maidstone, Kent, ME14 5XU
Great Britain, www.crmoon.com

CONTENTS

NOTE ON THE TEXT

The text is from *Dürer* by Herbert Furst, published by T.C. &
E.C. Jack, London and Frederick A. Stokes, New York, 1910 as
part of the Masterpieces In Colour series, edited by T. Leman
Hare.

The illustrations discussed in the book are included in the
illustrations section, along with many other works.

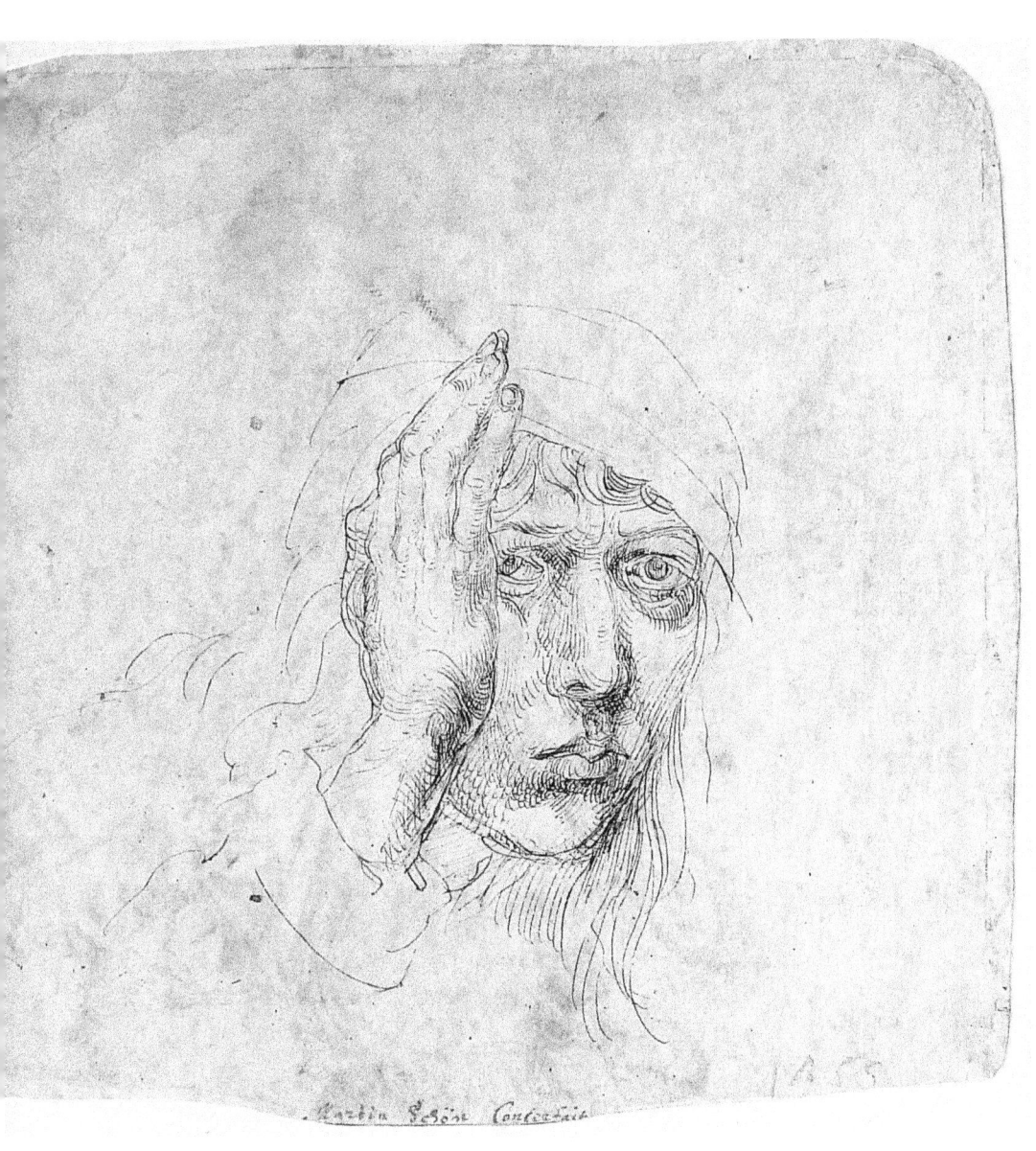

Albrecht Dürer, Self-Portrait, 1492, Erlangen

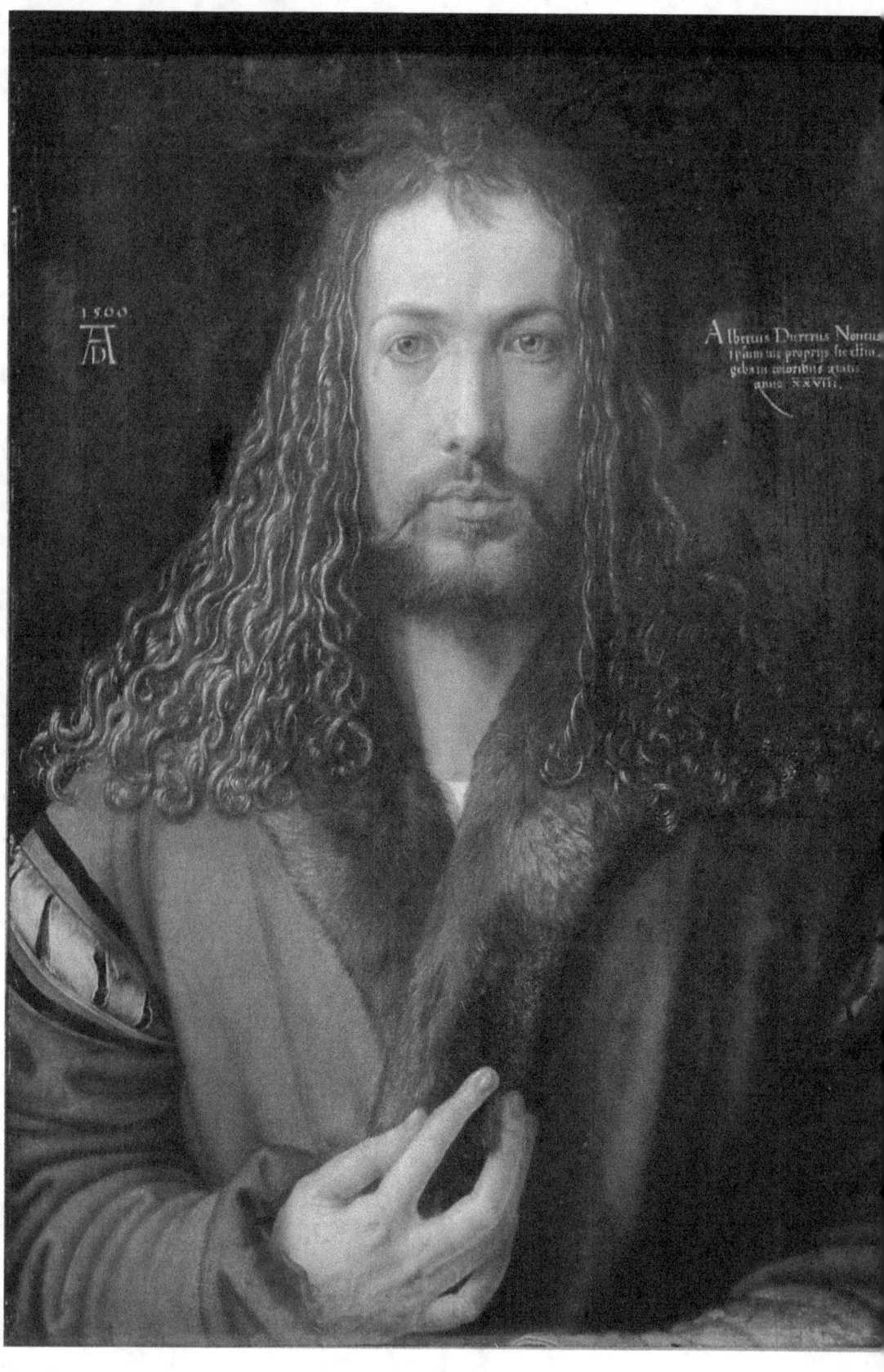

Albrecht Dürer, Self-Portrait, Munich

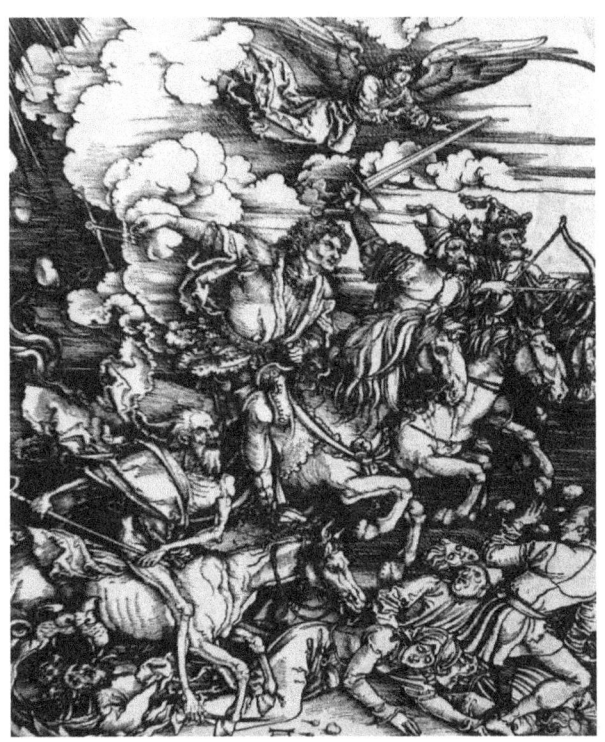

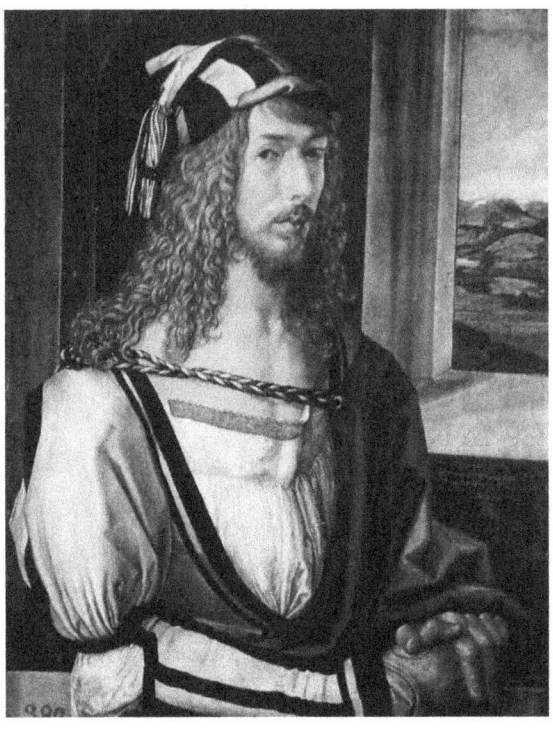

Albrecht Dürer

THIS is a wonderful world! And not the least wonderful thing is our ignorance of it.

I would chat with you, reader, for a while; would discuss Dürer, whom I have known and loved for many a year, and whom I want to make beloved by you also. Here I sit, pen in hand, and would begin.

Begin – where?

With the Beginnings?

The Beginnings? Where do things begin; when and why?

So our ignorance, like a many-headed monster, raises its fearsome heads and would bar the way.

By most subtle links are all things connected – cause and effect we call them; and if we but raise one or the other, fine ears will hear the clinking – and the monster rises.

There are so many things we shall never know, cries the poet of the unsaid, Maeterlinck.

Let us venture forth then and grope with clumsy fingers amongst the treasures stored; let us be content to pick up a jewel here and there, resting our minds in awe and admiration on its beauty, though we may not readily understand its use and meaning. Foolish men read books and dusty documents, catch a few dull words from the phrasing of long thoughts, and will tell you, these are facts!

Wise men read books – the books of Nature and the books of men – and say, facts are well enough, but oh for the right understanding!

For between sunrise and sunset, between the dusk of evening and the dusk of dawn, things happen that will never happen again; and the world of to-day is ever a world of yesterdays and to-morrows.

Reader, I lift my torch, and by its dim light I bid you follow me.

For it is a long journey we have to make through the night of the past. Many an encumbrance of four and a half centuries we shall have to lay aside ere we reach the treasure-house of Dürer's Art.

From the steps of Kaiser Wilhelm II.'s throne we must hasten through the ages to Kaiser Maximilian's city, Nuremberg – to the days when Wilhelm's ancestors were but Margraves of Brandenburg, scarcely much more than the Burggraves of Nuremberg they had originally been.

From the days of the Maxim gun and the Lee-Metford to the days of the howitzer and the blunderbuss. When York was farther away from London than New York is to-day.

When the receipt of a written letter was fact but few could boast of; and a secret *billet-doux* might cause the sender to be flung in gaol. When the morning's milk was unaccompanied by the morning news; for the printer's press was in its infancy.

When the stranding of a whale was an event of European interest, and the form of a rhinoceros the subject of wild conjecture and childish imagination.

When this patient earth of ours was to our ancestors merely a vast pancake toasted daily by a circling sun.

When the woods were full of hobgoblins, and scaly Beelzebubs were busily engaged in pitching the souls of the damned down a yawning hell-mouth, and the angels of the Lord in crimson and brocade carried the blessed heavenward. In those days scholars filled their books with a curious jumble of theology, philosophy, and old women's talk. Dr. Faustus practised black magic, and the besom-steeds carried witches from the Brocken far and wide into all lands.

Then no one ventured far from home unaccompanied, and the merchants were bold adventurers, and Kings of Scotland might envy Nuremberg burgesses – so Æneas Sylvius said.

And that a touch of humour be not lacking, I bid you

remember that my lady dipped her dainty fingers into the stew, and, after, threw the bare bones to the dogs below the table; and I also bid you remember that satins and fine linen oft clothed an unwashed body.

Cruel plagues, smallpox, and all manner of disease and malformations inflicted a far greater number than nowadays, and the sad ignorance of doctors brewed horrid draughts amongst the skulls, skeletons, stuffed birds, and crocodiles of their fearsome-looking "surgeries."

In short, it was a "poetic" age; when all the world was full of mysteries and possibilities, and the sanest and most level-headed were outrageously fantastic.

There are people who will tell you that the world is very much the same to-day as it was yesterday, and that, after all, human nature is human nature in all ages all the world over. But, beyond the fact that we all are born and we all must die, there is little in common between you and me – between us of to-day and those of yesterday – and we resemble each other most nearly in things that do not matter.

Frankly, therefore, Albrecht Dürer, who was born on May 21, 1471, is a human being from another world, and unless you realise that too, I doubt you can understand him, much less admire him.

For his Art is not beautiful.

Germans have never been able to create anything beautiful in Art: their sense of beauty soars into Song.

But even whilst I am writing these words it occurs to me that they are no longer true, for the German of to-day is no longer the German of yesterday, "standing peaceful on his scientific watch-tower; and to the raging, struggling multitude here and elsewhere solemnly, from hour to hour, with preparatory blast of cow-horn emit his 'Höret ihr Herren und lasst's euch sagen' …" as Carlyle pictures him; he is most certainly not like the Lutheran German with a child's heart and a boy's rash courage.

Frankly I say you cannot admire Dürer if you be honestly

ignorant or ignorantly honest.

We of to-day are too level-headed; our brains cannot encompass the world that crowded Dürer's dreams.

For the German's brain was always crowded; he had not that nice sense of space and emptiness that makes Italian Art so pleasant to look upon, and which the Japanese employ with astonishing subtlety. You remember Wagner's words in Goethe's "Faust" –

"Zwar weiss ich viel; doch möcht ich Alles wissen."
(I know a lot, yet wish that I knew All.)

It is not only his eagerness to show you all he knows, but also his ravenous desire to know all that is to be known. Hence we speak of German thoroughness, at once his boast and his modesty.

Here again I have to pull up. Generalisations are so easy, appear so justified, and are more often than not misleading.

Dürer was not a pure-blooded Teuton; his father came from Eytas in Hungary.[1]

That German music owes a debt of gratitude to Hungary is acknowledged. Does Dürer owe his greatness to the strain of foreign blood?

Possibly; but it does not matter. He was a man, and a profound man, therefore akin to all the world, as Dante and Michelangelo, as Shakespeare and Millet. Born into German circumstances he appears in German habit – that is all.

His father Albrecht was a goldsmith, and Albrecht the son having shown himself worthy of a better education than his numerous brothers, was, after finishing school, apprenticed to and would have remained a goldsmith, had his artistic nature not drawn him to Art; at least so his biographer, *i.e.* the painter himself, tells us. It was not the artist alone who longed for freer play, for freer expression of his faculties. It was to a great extent, I

---

1 Eytas translated into German is Thür (Door), and a man from Thür a Thürer or Dürer.

feel sure, the thinker.

Dürer took himself tremendously seriously; were it not for some letters that he has left us, and some episodes in his graphic art, one might be led to imagine that Dürer knew not laughter, scarcely even a smile. He consequently thought it of importance to acquaint the world with all the details of his life and work, recording even the moods which prompted him to do this or that. In Dürer the desire to live was entirely absorbed in the desire to think. He was not a man of action, and the records of his life are filled by accounts of what he saw, what he thought, and what others thought of him; coupled with frequent complaints of jealousies and lack of appreciation. Dürer was deep but narrow, and in that again he reflects the religious spirit of Protestantism, not the wider culture of Humanism. His ego looms large in his consciousness, and it is the salvation of the soul rather than the expansion of the mind which concerns him; but withal he is like Luther – a *Man*.

His idea then of Art was, that it "should be employed," as he himself explained, "in the service of the Church to set forth the sufferings of Christ and such like subjects, and it should also be employed to preserve the features of men after their death." A narrow interpretation of a world-embracing realm.

The scope of this little volume will not admit of a detailed account of Dürer's life.

We may not linger on the years of his apprenticeship with Michael Wolgemut, where he suffered much from his fellow-'prentices. We must not accompany him on his wanderjahre, these being the three years of peregrination which always followed the years of apprenticeship.

Neither may we record details, as of his marriage with Agnes Frey – "mein Agnes," upon his return home in 1494. "His Agnes" was apparently a good housewife and a shrewd business woman, to whom he afterwards largely entrusted the sale of his prints.

He had a great struggle for a living. And here an amusing

analogy occurs to me. Painting does not pay, he complains at one time, and therefore he devotes himself to "black and white."

Was it ever thus? Would that some of our own struggling artists remembered Dürer, and even when they find themselves compelled to do something to keep the pot aboiling, at any rate do their best.

We have it on Dürer's own authority that he took up etching and wood-engraving because it paid better. And strange – into this bread-and-butter work he put his best.

It is not his painting that made his fame and name, though in that branch of Art he was admired by a Raphael and a Bellini.

Agnes Frey bore him no children; this fact, I think, is worthy of note. Even a cursory glance at Dürer's etchings and woodcuts will reveal the fact that he was fond of children – "kinderlieb," as the Germans say. I do not doubt that he would have given us even more joy and sunshine in his Art had he but called a child his own.

Instead, we have too often the gloomy reflection of death throughout his work. The gambols and frolics of angelic cupids are too often obscured by the symbols of suffering, sin, and death.

Again, we must not allow a logical conclusion to be accepted as an absolute truth.

Dürer was certainly more familiar with death and suffering than we are.

Unless the grey lady and the dark angel visit our own homes, most of us – of my readers, at any rate – have to seek deliberately the faces of sorrow in the slums and the grimaces of death in the Coroner's Court. But in Dürer's days death lurked beyond the city walls; the sight of the slain or swinging victims of knightly valour, and peasant's revenge, blanched the cheeks of many maidens, and queer plagues and pestilences mowed the most upright to the ground. The Dance of Death was a favourite subject with the old painters, not because their disposition was morbid, but because the times were more out of joint than they are now.

All these points have to be realised before one can hope to

understand Dürer even faintly. Again, when we examine more closely the apparently quaint and fantastic form his mode of visualising takes, we must make allowances for the habits and customs and costumes of the times – as indeed one has to, in the case of all old masters, and for which reason I humbly submit that the study of old masters properly belongs to the few, not the many. A great deal of erroneous opinions are held simply because it is difficult to disentangle the individual from the typical.

Dürer, whose wanderjahre had taken him to Strasburg and Bâle and Venice, returned home again apparently uninfluenced.

Critics from Raphael's age down to the last few years have lamented this fact; have thought that "knowledge of classic antiquity" might have made a better artist of him.

Now, Dürer was not an artist in its wider sense; he was a craftsman certainly, but above all a thinker. Dürer uses his eyes for the purposes of thought; he could close them without disturbing the pageants of his vision. But whereas we have no hint that his dreams were of beauty, we have every indication that they were literal transcriptions of literary thoughts. When he came to put these materialisations into the form of pictures or prints, the craftsman side, the practical side of his nature, resolved them into scientific problems, with the remarkable result that these visions are hung on purely materialistic facts. From our modern point of view Dürer was decidedly lacking in artistic imagination, which even such men as Goya and Blake, or "si parva licet comparere magnis" John Martin and Gustave Doré, and the delightful Arthur Rackham of our own times possess.

His importance was his craftsmanship, whilst the subject-matter of his pictures – the portraits excepted – and particularly of his prints, are merely of historic interest – "von kulturhistorischer Bedeutung," the German would say.

In 1506 and 1507 he visited Venice, as already stated, gracefully received by the nobles and Giovanni Bellini, but disliked by the other painters.

He returned home apparently uninfluenced by the great Venetians, Titian, remember, amongst them. Gentile Bellini and Vittore Carpaccio were then the only painters at Venice who saw the realistic side of Nature; but they were prosaic, whilst our Dürer imbued a wooden bench or a tree trunk with a personal and human interest. Those of my readers who can afford the time to linger on this aspect of Dürer's activity should compare Carpaccio's rendering of St. Jerome in his study with Dürer's engraving of the same subject.

Dürer the craftsman referred in everything he painted or engraved to Nature. But of course it was Nature as he and his times saw it; neither Hals, Rembrandt, neither Ribera, Velazquez, neither Chardin nor Constable, neither Monet nor Whistler had as yet begun to ascend the rungs of progress towards truthful – that is, "optical sight."

Dürer's reference to Nature means an intricate study of theoretical considerations, coupled with the desire to record everything he knew about the things he wished to reproduce.

His was an analytical mind, and every piece of work he produced is a careful dovetailing of isolated facts. Consequently his pictures must not be looked *at*, but looked *into* – must be *read*.

Again an obvious truth may here mislead us. The analytical juxtaposition of facts was a characteristic of the age. Dürer's Art was a step forward; he – like Raphael, like Titian – dovetailed, where earlier men scarcely joined. Dürer has as yet not the power that even the next generation began to acquire – he never suggests anything; he works everything out, down to the minutest details. There are no slight sketches of his but such as suggest great travail of sight, encumbranced by an over-thoughtful mind.

To understand Dürer you require time; each print of the "Passions," "The Life of Mary," the "Apokalypse," should be read like a page printed in smallest type, with thought and some eye-strain. That of course goes very much against the grain of our own age; we demand large type and short stories.

The study of his work entails considerable self-sacrifice. Your own likes and dislikes you have to suppress, and try to see with eyes that belong to an age long since gone. Do not despise the less self-sacrificing, who refuse the study of old Art; and distrust profoundly those others who laud it beyond measure. The green tree is the tree to water; the dead tree – be its black branches and sere leaves never so picturesque – is beyond the need of your attentions.

The Scylla and Charybdis of æsthetic reformers is praise of the old, and poor appraising of the new.

Now the old Italians thought Dürer a most admirable artist, blamed what they called the defects of his Art on the ungainliness of his models, and felt convinced that he might have easily been the first among the Italians had he lived there, instead of the first among the "Flemings." They were of course wrong, for it is the individual reflex-action of Dürer's brain which caused his Art to be what it is; in Italy it would still have been an individual reflex-action, and Dürer had been in Venice without the desired effect. Dürer might, however, himself seem to confirm the Italians' opinion: he strayed into the barren fields of theoretical speculations – barren because some of his best work was done before he had elaborated his system, barren because speculation saps the strength of natural perception. Dürer sought a "Canon of Beauty," and the history of Art has proved over and over again that beauty canonised is damned.

One more remark: his contemporaries and critics praised the extraordinary technical skill with which he could draw straight lines without the aid of a ruler, or the astounding legerdemain with which he reproduced every single hair in a curl – the "Paganini" worship which runs through all the ages; which in itself is fruitless; touches the fiddle-strings at best or cerebral cords, not heart-strings.

Out of all the foregoing, out of all the mortal and mouldering coverings we have now to shell the real, the immortal Dürer – the Dürer whose mind was longing for truth, whose soul was longing for harmony, and who out of his longings fashioned his Art, as all great men have done and will do until the last.

On the title-page of the "Small Passion" is a woodcut – the "Man of Sorrows."

There, reader, you have, in my opinion, the greatness of Dürer; he never surpassed it. It is the consciousness of man's impotence; it is the saddest sight mortal eyes can behold – that of a man who has lost faith in himself.

If Dürer were here now I am sure he would lay his hand upon my shoulder, and, his deep true eyes searching mine, his soft and human lips would say:-

You are right, my friend; this is my best, for it is the spirit of my age that spoke in me then.

In front of the Pantheon at Paris is a statue called The Thinker. A seated man, unconscious of his bodily strength, for all his consciousness is in the iron grip of thought. He looks not up, not down – he looks before him; and methinks, reader, I can hear an unborn voice proclaim:

This too was once the Spirit of an Age. Two milestones on the path of human progress; an idle fancy if you will – no more.

Of the Man of Sorrows then we spoke: It is a small thing, but done exceeding well, for in the simplicity of form it embraces a world of meaning; and whilst you cannot spare one iota from the words of the Passion, on account of this picture, yet all the words of Christ's suffering seem alive in this plain print. Could there be a better frontispiece?

In judging, not enjoying, a work of art, one should first make sure that one understands the methods of the artist; one should next endeavour to discover his evident purpose or aim, or "motif," and forming one's judgment, ask: Has the artist succeeded in welding aim and result into one organic whole?

Neither the "motif" nor its form are in themselves of value, but the harmony of both – hence we may place Dürer's "Man of Sorrows" by the side of Michelangelo's "Moses," as of equal importance, of equal greatness. This "Man of Sorrows" we must praise as immortal Art, and the reason is evident; Dürer, who designed it during an illness, had himself suffered and knew sorrow – *felt* what he visualised.

If we compare another woodcut, viz. the one from "Die heimliche Offenbarung Johannis," illustrating Revelations i. 12-17, we will have to draw a different conclusion. Let us listen to the passage Dürer set himself to illustrate:

> 12. And I turned to see the voice that spake with me. And being turned, I saw seven golden candlesticks;
> 13. And in the midst of the seven candlesticks one like unto the Son of man, clothed with a garment down to the foot, and girt about the paps with a golden girdle.
> 14. His head and hairs white like wool, as white as snow; and his eyes as a flame of fire;
> 15. And his feet like unto fine brass, as if they burned in a furnace; and his voice as the sound of many waters.
> 16. And he had in his right hand many stars: and out of his mouth went a sharp two-edged sword: and his countenance was as the sun shineth in his strength.
> 17. And when I saw him, I fell at his feet as dead.

Assuming that a passage such as this *can* be illustrated, and that without the use of colour, is his a good illustration? Does it reproduce the spirit and meaning of St. John, or only the words? Look at the two-edged sword glued to the mouth, look at the eyes "as a flame of fire"; can you admit more than that it pretends to be a literal translation? But it is not even literal; verse 17 says distinctly, "And when I saw him, I fell at his feet as dead." But St. John is here represented as one praying. Then what is the inference? That Dürer was unimaginative in the higher sense of the word; that he, like the Spirit of the Reformation, sought salvation in the WORD. Throughout Dürer's Art we feel that it was constrained, hampered by his inordinate love of literal truthfulness; not one of his works ever rises even to the level of Raphael's "Madonna della Seggiola." Like German philosophy, his works are so carefully elaborated in detail that the glorious whole is lost in more or less warring details. His Art suffers from insubordination – all facts are co-ordinated. He himself knew it, and towards the end of this life hated its complexity, caused by the desire to represent in one picture the successive development of the spoken or written word; a desire which even in our days has not completely disappeared.

Dürer therefore appeals to us of to-day more through such conceptions as the wings of the Paumgaertner altar-piece, or the four Temperaments (St. Peter, St. John, St. Mark, and St. Paul), than through the crowded centre panels of his altar-pieces; and the strong appeal of his engravings, such as the "Knight of the Reformation" (1513) or the "Melancholia" (1514), is mainly owing to the predominant big note of the principal figures, whilst in the beautiful St. Jerome ("Hieronymus im Gehäus") it is the effect of sunshine and its concomitant feeling of well-being – *Gemüthlichkeit*, to use an untranslatable German word – which makes us linger and dwell with growing delight on every detail of this wonderful print.

In spite of appearances to the contrary, Dürer was, as I have said, unimaginative. He needed the written word or another's idea as a guide; he never dreamt of an Art that could be beautiful without a "mission" – he never "created." Try to realise for a moment that throughout his work – in accordance with the conception of his age – he mixes purely modern dress with biblical and classical representation, as if our Leightons, Tademas, Poynters, were to introduce crinolines, bustles, or "empire" gowns amongst Venuses and Apollos. In the pathetic "Deposition from the Cross" the Magdalen is just a "modern" Nuremberg damsel, and the Virgin's headwrap is slung as the northern housewife wore it, and not like an Oriental woman's; Joseph of Arimathea and Nicodemus are clad as Nuremberg burghers, and only in the figure of John does he make concession to the traditional "classic" garment. Such an anachronistic medley could only appear logical so long as the religious spirit and the convictions of the majority were at one. I dare scarcely hint at, much less describe, the feelings that would be stirred in you if a modern painter represented the Crucifixion with Nicodemus and the man from Arimathea in frock-coats, Mary and the Magdalen in "walking costume," and a company of Horse-guards in attendance. The abyss of over four centuries divides us from Dürer; my suggestion sounds blasphemous almost, yet it is a thought based on fact and worthy of most careful note.

Owing to a convention – then active, now defunct – Dürer grasped the hands of all the living, bade them stop and think. Not one of those who beheld his work could pass by without feeling a call of sympathy and understanding. "Everyman" Dürer! – that is his grandeur. To this the artists added their appreciation; what he did was not only *truly* done, but on the testimony of all his brothers in Art *well* done. So with graver, pen, and brush he gave his world the outlines of Belief. In his pictures the illiterate saw, as by revelation, that which they could not read, and the literate, the literati – Erasmus, Pirkheimer, Melanchthon amongst the most prominent – saw the excellence of the manner of his revelations.

I cannot think of any better way of explaining the effect of Dürer's Art as an illustrator upon his time, than to beg you to imagine the delight a short-sighted man experiences when he is given his first pair of spectacles. Everything remains where it is; he has not lost his sense of orientation, but on a sudden he sees everything more clearly, more defined, more in detail: and where he previously had only recognised vague effects he begins to see their causes. Such was the effect of Dürer's Art: features, arms, hands, bodies, legs, feet, draperies, accessories, tree-trunks and foliage, vistas, radiance and light, not suggested but present, truly realised. When I say Dürer was not imaginative I mean to convey that imagination was characteristic of the age, not of him alone, but the materialisation, the realisation of fancy, that is his strength.

All these considerations can find, unfortunately, no room for discussion in these pages, for it were tedious to refer the reader to examples which are not illustrated.

We must perforce accept the limitations of our programme, and devote our attention to his paintings – far the least significant part of his activity.

Dürer was the great master of line – he thinks in line. This line is firstly the outline or contour in its everyday meaning; secondly, it is the massed army of lines that go to make shadow; thirdly, it is line in its psychical aspect, as denoting direction, aim, tendency, such as we have it in the print of the "Melancholia." No one before him had ever performed such wonderful feats with "line," not even Mantegna with his vigorous but repellent parallels.

This line was the greatest obstacle to his becoming a successful painter. For his line was not the great sweep, not the graceful flow, not the spontaneous dash, not the slight touch, but the heavy, determined, reasoned move, as of a master-hand in a game of chess.

To him, consequently, the world and his Art were problems, not joys.

Consider one of his early works – the portrait of his father, the honest, God-fearing, struggling goldsmith. The colour of this work is monotonous, a sort of gold-russet. It might almost be a monochrome, for the interest is centred in the wrinkles and lines of care and old age with which Father Time had furrowed the skin of the old man, and which Dürer has imitated with the determination of a ploughshare cleaving the glebe.

When we come to his subject pictures, we will have to notice at once that they have been constructed, not felt. It has been remarked that Dürer did for northern Art, or at least attempted, what Leonardo did for Italian Art, viz., converted empirical Art into a theoretical science. Whether such conversion was not in reality a perversion, is a question that cannot be discussed here. We have, at any rate, in Dürer a curious example of an artist referring to Nature in order to discard it; the idealist become realist in order to further his idealism. Most of his pictures contain statements of pictorial facts which are in themselves most true, but taken in conjunction with the whole picture quite untrue. Dürer lacked the courage to trust his sense of sight, his optic organ: beauty with him is a thing which must be thought out, not seen. Dürer had come into direct contact with Italian Art, had felt himself a gentleman in Venice, and only a "parasite" in Nuremberg. From Italy he imported a conception of beauty which really was quite foreign to him. Italy sowed dissension in his mind, for he was ever after bent on finding a formula of beauty, which he could have dispensed with had he remained the simple painter as we know him in his early self-portrait of 1493. There can be no doubt that Dürer was principally looking towards Italy for approval, as indeed he had little reason to cherish the opinions of the painters in his own country, who were so greatly his inferiors both in mind as in their Art.

Much has been made of the fact that painting was a "free" Art, not a "Guild" in Nuremberg. Now carpentering was also a "free" Art at Nuremberg, and painting was not "free" in Italy, so the glory of freedom is somewhat discounted; but whatever Art was, Dürer, at any rate, was not an artist in Raphael's, Bellini's, or Titian's sense. He was pre-eminently a thinker, a moralist, a scientist, a searcher after absolute truth, seeking expression in Art. Once this is realised his pictures make wonderfully good reading.

The "Deposition," for example, is full of interest. The dead Christ, whose still open lips have not long since uttered "Into Thy hands, O Lord," is being gently laid on the ground, His poor pierced feet rigid, the muscles of His legs stiff as in a cramp. The Magdalen holds the right hand of the beloved body, and the stricken mother of Christ is represented in a manner almost worthy of the classic Niobe. Wonderfully expressive, too, are all the hands in this picture. Dürer found never-ending interest in the expressiveness of the hand. But if we were to seek in his colour any beauty other than intensity, we should be disappointed, as we should for the matter of that in any picture painted before the advent of Titian.

Again that monster Ignorance stirs. For as I speak of colour, as

I dogmatise on Titian, I am aware that colour may mean so many different things, and any one who wished to contradict me would be justified in doing so, not because I am wrong and he is right, but because of my difficulty in explaining colour, and his natural wish to aim at my vulnerable spot. Because I am well-nigh daily breaking bread with painters who unconsciously reveal the workings of their mind to me, I know that all the glibly used technical terms of their Art are as fixed as the colour of a chameleon. Different temperaments take on different hues. There is colour in Van Eyck and Crivelli, in Bellini and Botticelli, but deliberate colour harmonies, though arbitrary in choice, belong to Titian.

Dürer is no colourist, because, as we have already said, painting was the problem, not the joy of expression – in that he is Mantegna's equal, and Beato Angelico's inferior.

Thus looking on the "Madonna mit dem Zeisig" at Berlin, we may realise its beauty with difficulty. For whatever it may have been to his contemporaries, to us it means little, by the side of the splendid Madonnas from Italy, or even compared with his own engraved work.

This "Madonna with the Siskin" is a typical Dürer. In midst of the attempted Italian repose and "beauty" of the principal figures, we have the vacillating, oscillating profusion of Gothic detail. The fair hair of the Madonna drawn tightly round the head reappears in a gothic mass of crimped curls spread over her right shoulder. On her left hangs a piece of ribbon knotted and twisted. The cushion on which the infant Saviour sits is slashed, laced, and tassled. The Infant holds a prosaic "schnuller" or baby-soother in His right hand, whilst the siskin is perched on the top of His raised forearm. Of the wreath-bearing angels, one displays an almost bald head, and the background is full of unrest. Even the little label bearing the artist's name, by which old masters were wont to mark their pictures, and which in Bellini's case, for instance, appears plain and flatly fixed, bends up, like the little films of gelatine, which by their movements are thought to betray the holder's temperament.

One of the tests of great Art is its appearance of inevitableness: in that the artist vies with the creator:

"The Moving Finger writes, and having writ,
Moves on; nor all your piety nor wit
Shall lure it back to cancel half a line."

There are a good many "lines" in the "Siskin" Madonna which bear cancelling: not one in the Madonna of the title-page of the "Marieenleben," which for that reason is a work of greater Art.

The fact is, that whilst his engraved and black and white work reaches at times monumental height, great in *saecula saeculorum*, there are too few of his painted pictures that have the power to arrest the attention of the student of Art, who must not be confounded with the student of Art-history.

As a painter he is essentially a primitive; as a graver he overshadows all ages.

Thus we see his great pictures one after the other: his Paumgaertner altar-piece, his "Deposition" – both in Munich; "The Adoration of the Magi" in the Uffizi; the much damaged but probably justly famed "Rosenkranz fest" in Prague, with his own portrait and that of his friend Pirckheimer in the background, and Emperor Max and Pope Julius II. in the foreground; the Dresden altar-piece, or the "Crucifixion," with the soft body of the crucified Christ and the weirdly fluttering loin-cloth; the strangely grotesque "Christ as a Boy in the Temple" in the Barberini Palace; the "Adam and Eve"; the "Martyrdom of the 10,000 Christians" – thus, I say, we see them one after the other pass before us, and are almost unmoved.

True, the Paumgaertner altar-piece has stirred us on account of the wing-pictures, but there is good reason for that, and we will revert to this reason later. The "Adoration of the Magi" seems reminiscent of Venetian influence. Not until we reach the year 1511 do we encounter a work that must arrest the attention of even the most indolent: it is the "Adoration of the Holy Trinity," or the All Saints altar-piece, painted for Matthew Landauer, whom we recognise, having seen Dürer's drawing of his features, in the man with the long nose on the left of the picture. This picture is without a doubt the finest, the greatest altar picture ever painted by any German. It is not by any means a large picture, measuring only 4 ft. 3 in. x 3 ft. 10-3/4 in., but it is so large in conception that it might well have been designed to cover a whole wall. Dürer has here surpassed himself; he has for once conceived with the exuberance of a Michelangelo, for it is more serious than a Raphael, it is less poetic than a Fra Angelico: but personally I state my conviction, that if ever all the Saints shall unite in adoration of the Trinity, this is the true and only possibility, this is instinct with verisimilitude, this might be taken for "documentary evidence." This communion of saints was beholden by man. If ever a man was a believer irrespective of Church, Creed, or sect – Dürer was he. I confess to a sense of awe in beholding this work, akin to Fra Angelico in its sincerity, akin to Michelangelo in its grandeur, and German wholly in the naturalness of its mystery. With more than photographic sharpness and minuteness of detail does Dürer materialise the vision: God-Father, an aged King – a Charlemagne; God-Son, the willing sufferer; the Holy Ghost, the dove of Sancgrael; the Heavenly Hosts above; the Saints beside and below – Saints that have lived and suffered, and are now assembled in praise – for the crowd is a living, praying, praising, and jubilant crowd.

Well might the creator of this masterpiece portray himself, and proudly state on the tablet he is holding:

Albertus Dürer Noricus faciebat.

This picture is not a vision – it is the statement of a dogmatic truth; as such it is painted with all the subtlety of doctrinal reasoning; not a romantic vision, nor a human truth, such as we find in Rembrandt's religious works. It is a ceremonial picture, only the ceremony is full, not empty; full of conviction, reverence, and faith! Such pictures are rare amongst Italians – in spite of all their sense of beauty; more frequent amongst the trans-alpine peoples, but never built in so much harmony. Unfortunately it has suffered, and is no longer in its pristine condition; it were fruitless therefore to discuss the merits of its colour.

Mindful of my intention only to pick up a jewel here and there, I will not weary the reader with the enumeration of his altar-pieces, Nativities, Entombments, Piétàs and Madonnas. I can do this with an easy mind, because in my opinion (and you, reader, have contracted by purchase to accept my guidance) his religious paintings are of historical rather than Art interest.

The "Adams and Eves" of the Uffizi and the Prado cannot rouse my enthusiasm either. In these pictures Dürer makes an attempt to create something akin to Dr. Zamenhof's Esperanto; a universal standard for the language of Art in the one case, of Life in the other: and in either case this language, laboriously and admirably constructed but lacking in vitality, leaves the heart untouched. Dürer's attempts to paint a classical subject, such as Hercules slaying the Stymphalian birds, are unsatisfying. I cannot see any beauty of conception in a timid and illogical mixture of realism and phantasy – it is not whole-hearted enough. Even Rembrandt's ridiculous "Rape of Ganymede" has reason and Art on his side. Imagination was not Dürer's "forte"; it is therefore with all the greater pleasure that we turn to his portraits.

Portraits are always more satisfactory than subject pictures, a fact which is particularly noticeable to-day. There are scores of painters whose portrait-painting is considerably more impressive than their subject-painting – not because portrait-painting is less difficult, but because it is more difficult to detect the weaknesses of painting in a portrait.

From the early Goethe-praised self portrait of 1493 down to the wonderful portraits of 1526 there are but few that are not rare works of Art, and of the few quite a goodly proportion may not be genuine at all.

Dürer's ego loomed large in his consciousness, and therefore, unlike Rembrandt (who also painted his own likeness time and again, though only for practice), Dürer was really proud of his person – as to be sure he had reason to be.

The portrait of 1493 shows us the young Dürer, who was in all probability betrothed to his "Agnes"; he is holding the emblem of Fidelity – Man's Troth as it is called in German – which on Goethe's authority I may explain is "Eryngo," or *anglice* Sea-holly, in his hand.

Five years later this same Dürer, having probably returned from Venice, appears in splendid array, a true gentleman, gloved, and his naturally wavy hair crisply crimped, clad in a most fantastic costume.

As his greatest portrait the Munich one, dated 1500, has always been acclaimed. His features here bear a striking resemblance to the traditional face of Christ, and no doubt the resemblance was intentional. The nose, characterised in other pictures by the strongly raised bridge, loses this disfigurement in its frontal aspect. There is an almost uncanny expression of life in his eyes; dark ages of Byzantine belief and Art spring to the mind, and compel the spectator into an attitude of reverence not wholly due to the merits of the painting.

The comparison with Holbein's work naturally obtrudes itself, when Dürer's portraits are the subject of discussion.

In the Wallace collection is a most delightful little miniature portrait of Holbein, by his own hand. Compare the two heads. What a difference! Holbein the craftsman *par excellence*; the man to whom drawing came as easily as seeing comes to us. With shrewd, cold, weighing eyes he sizes himself up in the mirror. He, too, is a man of knowledge; he does his work faithfully and exceedingly well, but leaves it there. He never moralises, draws no conclusions, infers nothing, states merely facts – and if the truth must be said, is the greater craftsman.

Dürer's mind was deeper; one might say the springs of his talent welling upwards had to break through strata of cross-lying thought, reaching his hand after much tribulation, and teaching it to set down all he knew.

So the Paumgaertner portraits, at one time supposed to represent Ulrich von Hutten and Franz von Sickingen – the Reformation knights – show a marvellous grasp of character, wholly astonishing in the unconventional attitude, whilst the portrait of his aged master, Michael Wohlgemut, overstates in its anxiety not to understate.

His portrait of Kaiser Maximilian, quiet, dignified, is yet somewhat small in conception.

Two years later, however, he painted a portrait now in the Prado, representing presumably the Nuremberg patrician, Hans Imhof the Elder.

Purely technically considered this picture appears to be immeasurably above his own portrait of 1500, and above any other excepting the marvellous works of 1526. Whoever this Hans Imhof was, Dürer has laid bare his very soul. These later portraits show that Dürer stood on the threshold of the modern world.

Hieronymus Holzschuer is another of Dürer's strikingly successful efforts to portray both form and mind, and although the colour of the man's face is of a conventional pink, yet the pale blue background, the white hair, the pink flesh, and the glaring eyes stamp themselves indelibly on the mind of the beholder, much to the detriment of the other picture in the Berlin Gallery, Jacob Muffel. Jacob Muffel, contrary to Jerome Holzschuer, looks a miser, a hypocrite, and the more unpleasant, as he does not by any means look a fool. But Dürer's craftsmanship here exceeds that of the Holzschuer portrait, whom we love for the sake of his display of white hair and flaming eyes. The enigma to me is how a man who had painted the three last portraits mentioned, could have fallen to the level of the "Madonna with the Apple" of the same year.

The finest portrait under his name is the "Portrait of a Woman" at Berlin. This indeed is a brilliant piece of portraiture, absolutely modern in feeling, exceeding Holbein; and unless my eyes, which have not rested upon its surface for over ten years, deceive me, it is quite unlike any portrait painted by him before – the nearest perhaps being the man's portrait at Munich of 1507. The picture is supposed to show Venetian influence, and might therefore belong to this epoch; but, to my thinking, documentary evidence alone could make this picture in its not Dürer-like mode of seeing an undoubted work from his hand.

Space forbids further enumeration, further discussion of his work. As to details of his biography the reader will find in almost every library some reliable records of his life, and several inexpensive books have also appeared of recent years.

Dürer's life was in reality uneventful. He died suddenly on April 6, 1528, in Nuremberg, having in all probability laid the foundations of his illness on his celebrated journey into Flanders in 1520-21, where he was fêted everywhere, and right royally received both by the civic authorities and his own brothers of the palette.

His stay at Venice as a young man, and this last-mentioned journey, were the greatest adventures of his body. His mind was ever adventurous, seeking new problems, overcoming new difficulties. It is so tempting to liken him to his own "Jerome in his Study," yet St. Jerome's life was the very antithesis of our Dürer. In Dürer there was nothing of the "Faust-Natur," as the Germans are fond of expressing an ill-balanced, all-probing mind. Dürer's moral equilibrium was upheld by his deep and sincere religious convictions. He is firmly convinced that God has no more to say to humanity than the Bible records. Dürer's difficulties end where Faust's began.

The last years of Dürer's life were spent in composing books on the theory and practice of Art.

To write an adequate "Life of Dürer" then is impossible in so small a compass. And if anything I said were wise, it were surely the fact that I wanted you, reader, in the very beginning to expect no more than a dim light on the treasure store of Dürer's Thought and Dürer's Art.

But however dim the light, I hope it has been a true light.

And here my conscience smites me! All along I may have appeared querulous, seeking to divulge Dürer's limitations rather than his excellences.

Perhaps! There are so many misconceptions about Dürer. He was a deep-thinking man; he was like the churches of the North – narrow, steep, dimly religious within, full of traceries, lacework, gargoyles, and grotesques without.

I have read that it used to be said in Italy: All the cities of Germany were blind, with the exception of Nuremberg, which was one-eyed. True! True also of Dürer and German Art.

In 1526, two years before his death, Dürer presented a panel to his native city, now cut in two, robbed of its Protestant inscription, and hanging in the Alte Pinakothek at Munich. Dürer's last great work!

It is as though he felt that the divine service of his life was drawing to its close. His life and Art I have likened to a Gothic Cathedral; his last works were as the closed wings of a gigantic altar-piece, before which he leaves posterity gazing overawed.

The life-size figures of this great work represent the four Apostles: St. John in flaming red, with St. Peter, St. Mark in white, with St. Paul.

Dürer's greatest work: here for once his mind and his hand were at one.

Menacing, colossal in conception these figures rise, simple with the simplicity Dürer aimed for, and at last attained; Byzantine in their awe-inspiring grandeur. But instead of the splendour of Byzantine gold he places his figures upon a jet-black ground, as if he wished to instil the knowledge that there is no light except that which the four Apostles reflect. He had said as much indeed himself years ago. These four figures, "painted with greater care than any other," are his artistic last will and testament. In the letter, by which he humbly begs acceptance of these pictures from the Council, he quotes the words of the four Apostles, which his pictures illustrate, viz:–

St. Peter, in his second epistle in the second chapter.

St. John, in the first epistle in the fourth chapter.

St. Paul, in the second epistle to Timothy in the third chapter.

St. Mark, in his Gospel in the twelfth chapter.

Read them and behold: The Book and the sword! The religion of love in Saracenic fierceness. The menacing guardians of the Word.

Dürer with finality excludes the faithless from all hope. It is this finality, this absolute faith in the Word, this firm conviction of the finiteness of all things, which characterise the whole of his Art. The spirit which brooks no uncertainty and suffers no metaphor, glues a veritable sword to the lips of the "Son of man."

This finality is the cause of Dürer's isolation. He has no followers in the world of creative *Art*. Close the doors of Dürer's cathedral and the world rolls on, rolls by unheeding.

After Dürer and Luther had gone – Luther, on whose behalf Dürer uttered so touching a prayer – Germany, the holy empire, fell upon evil times. After the death of Maximilian the fields of the cloth of gold and the fields of golden harvest were turned into rude jousting places of ruder rabble. The hand of time was set back for centuries.

We have a shrewd suspicion that Carlyle's German, with his cowhorn blasts, did not tell the universe "what o'clock it really is." We have a shrewd suspicion that in the beginning of last century the clocks in Germany had only just begun ticking after centuries of rest.

I am straying, reader.

What was it that Dürer had inscribed on the Apostle Panels?

"All worldly rulers in these times of danger should beware that they receive not false Teaching for the Word of God. For God will have nothing added to His Word nor yet taken away. Hear, therefore, these four excellent men, Peter, John, Paul, and Mark, their warning."

The narrow outlook of his time speaks here!

For words which bear addition or suffer subtraction, can never be the words of God.

God's words are worlds. Our words are stammerings, scarcely articulate.

Reader! look you, my torch burns dimly; let us back unto the day.

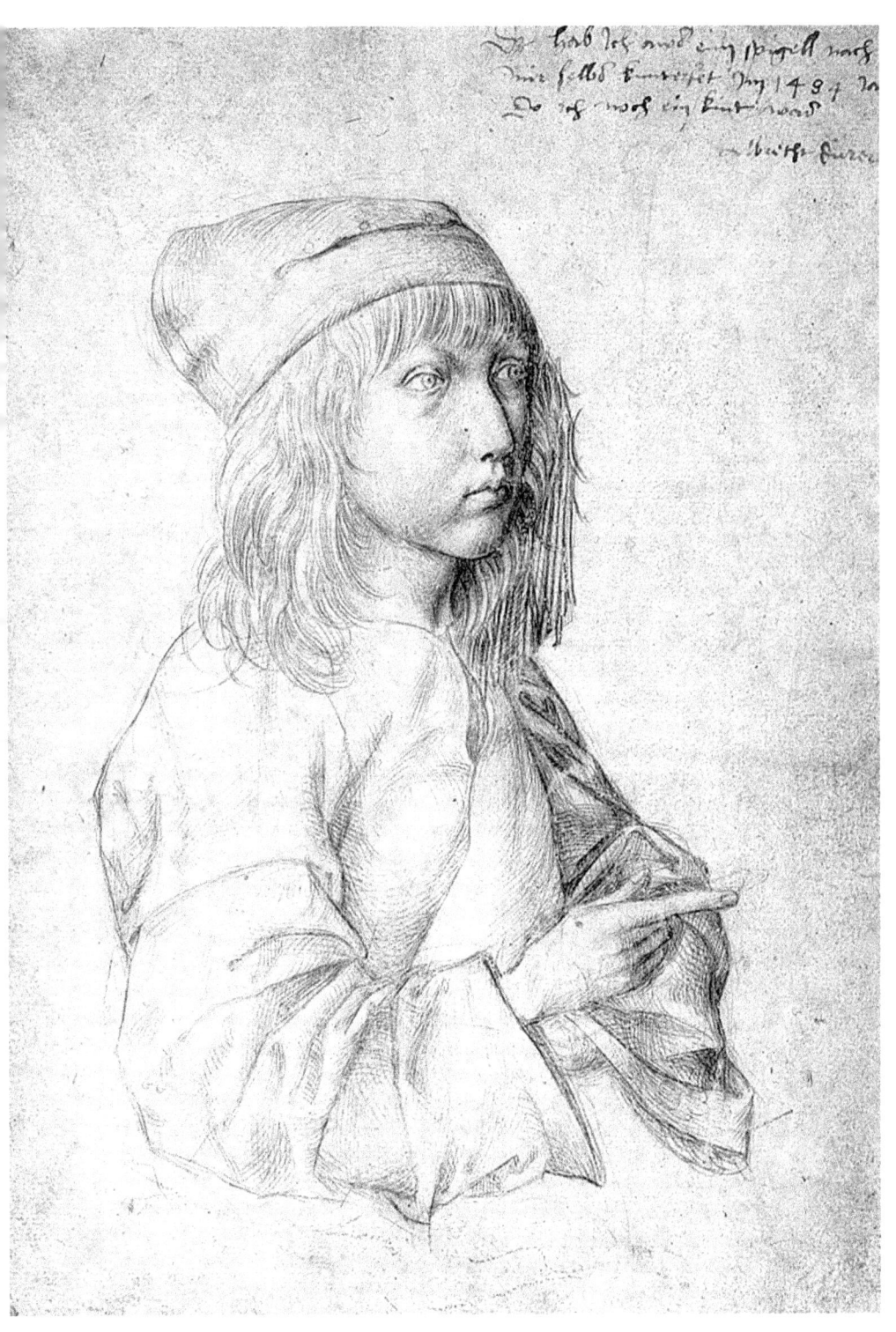

Albrecht Dürer, Self-Portrait At the Age of Thirteen, 1484, Vienna

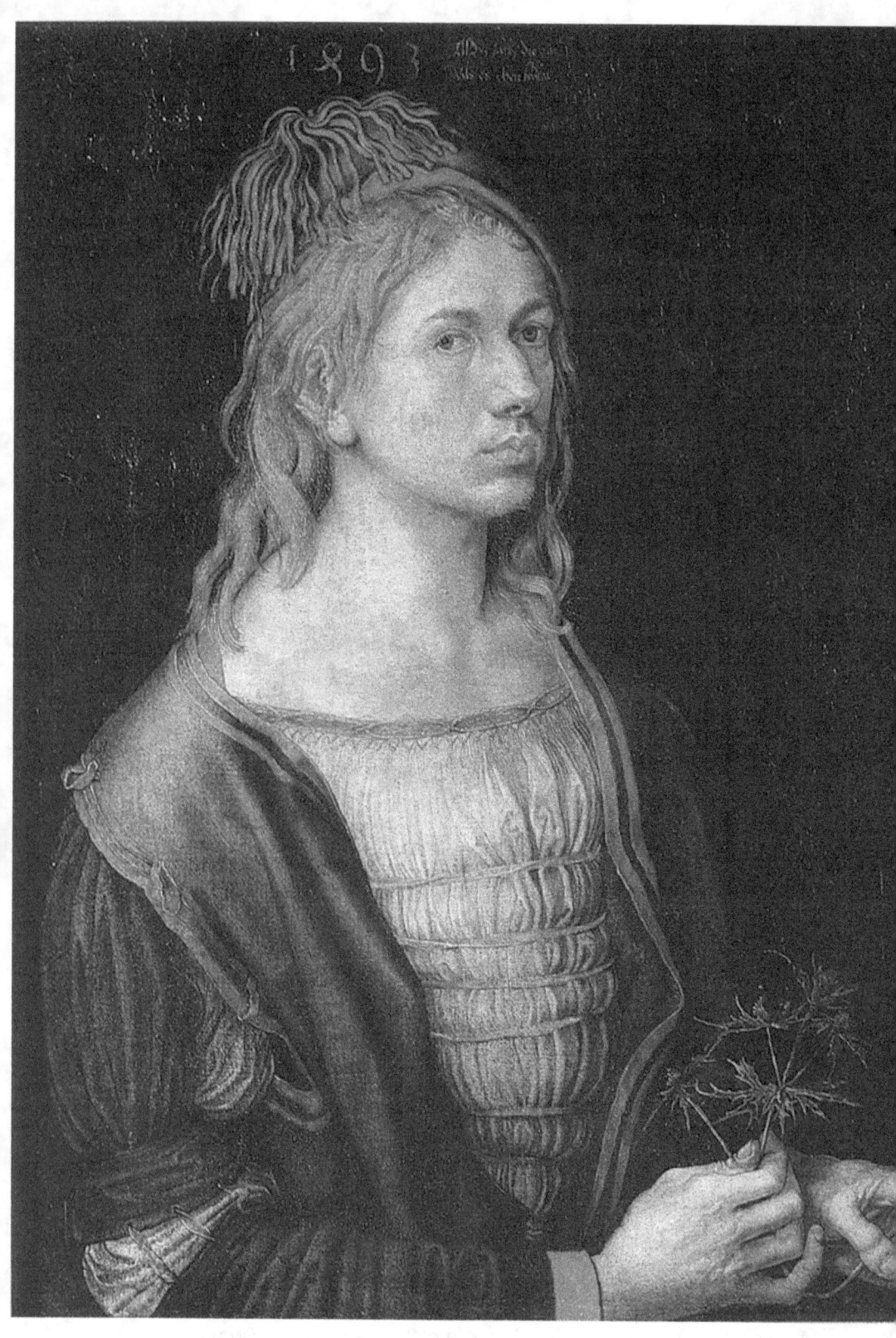

Albrecht Dürer, Self-Portrait, 1493 Louvre, Paris

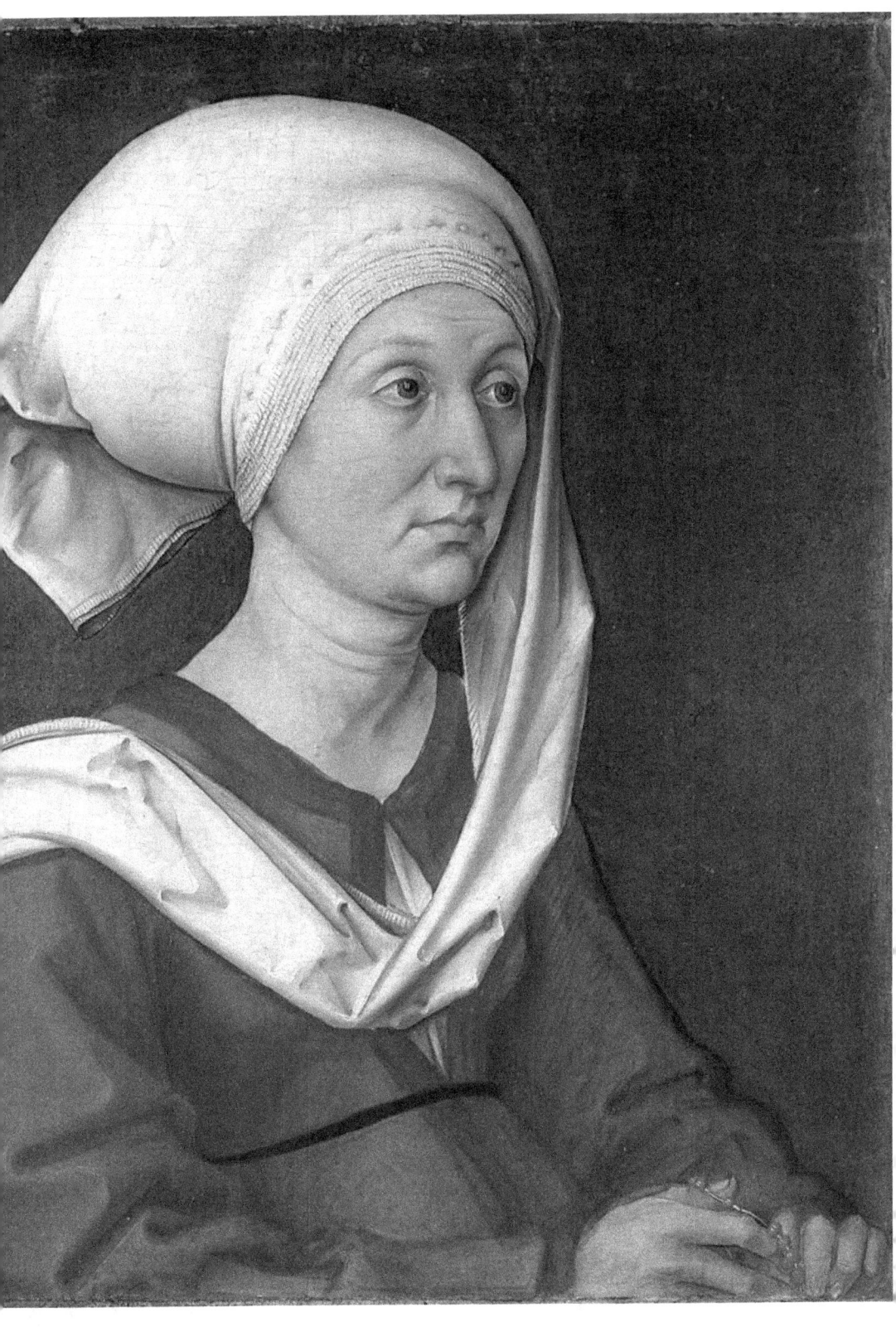

Albrecht Dürer, Portrait of His Mother, 1490, Nuremburg

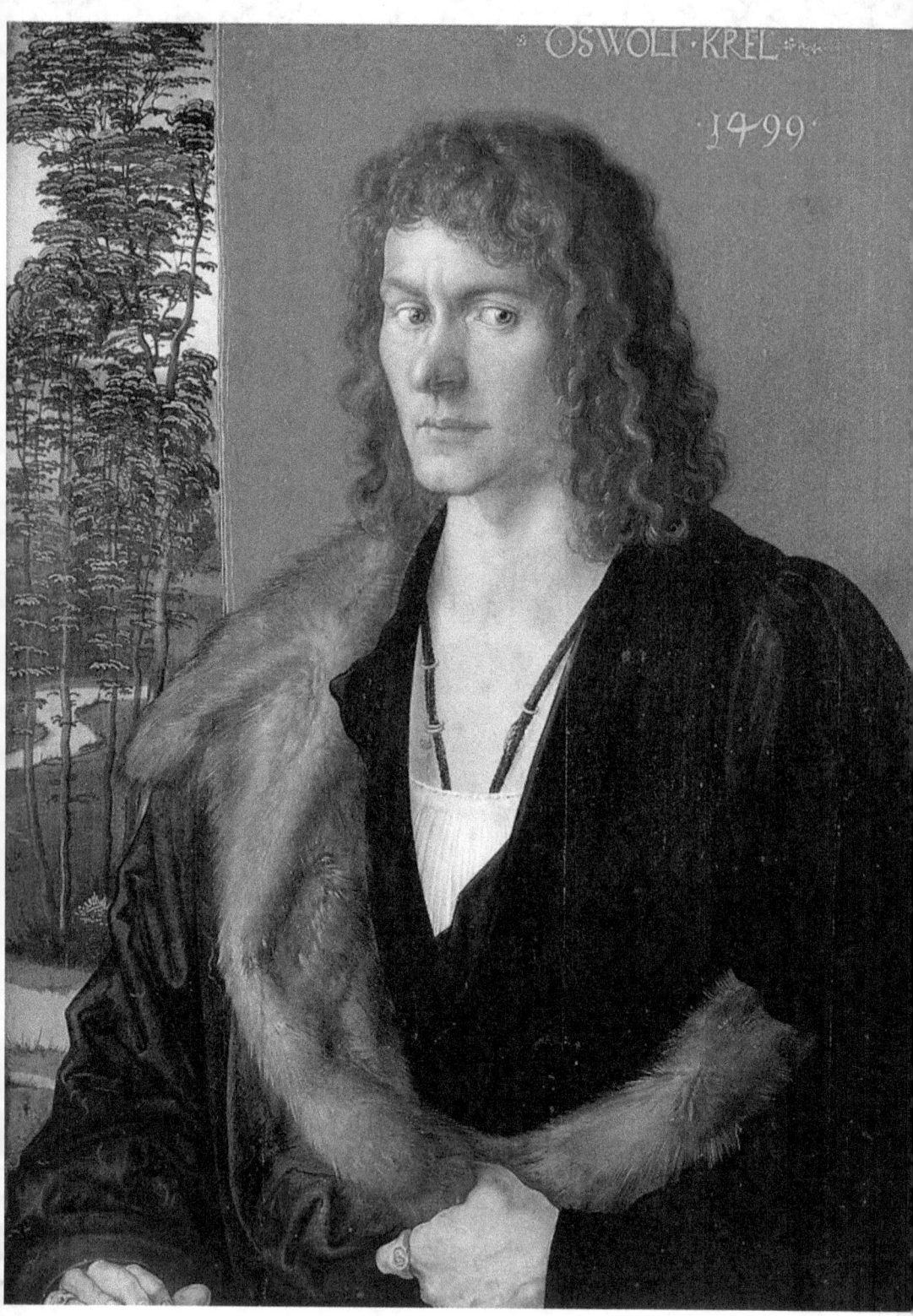

Albrecht Dürer, Oswolt Krel, 1499

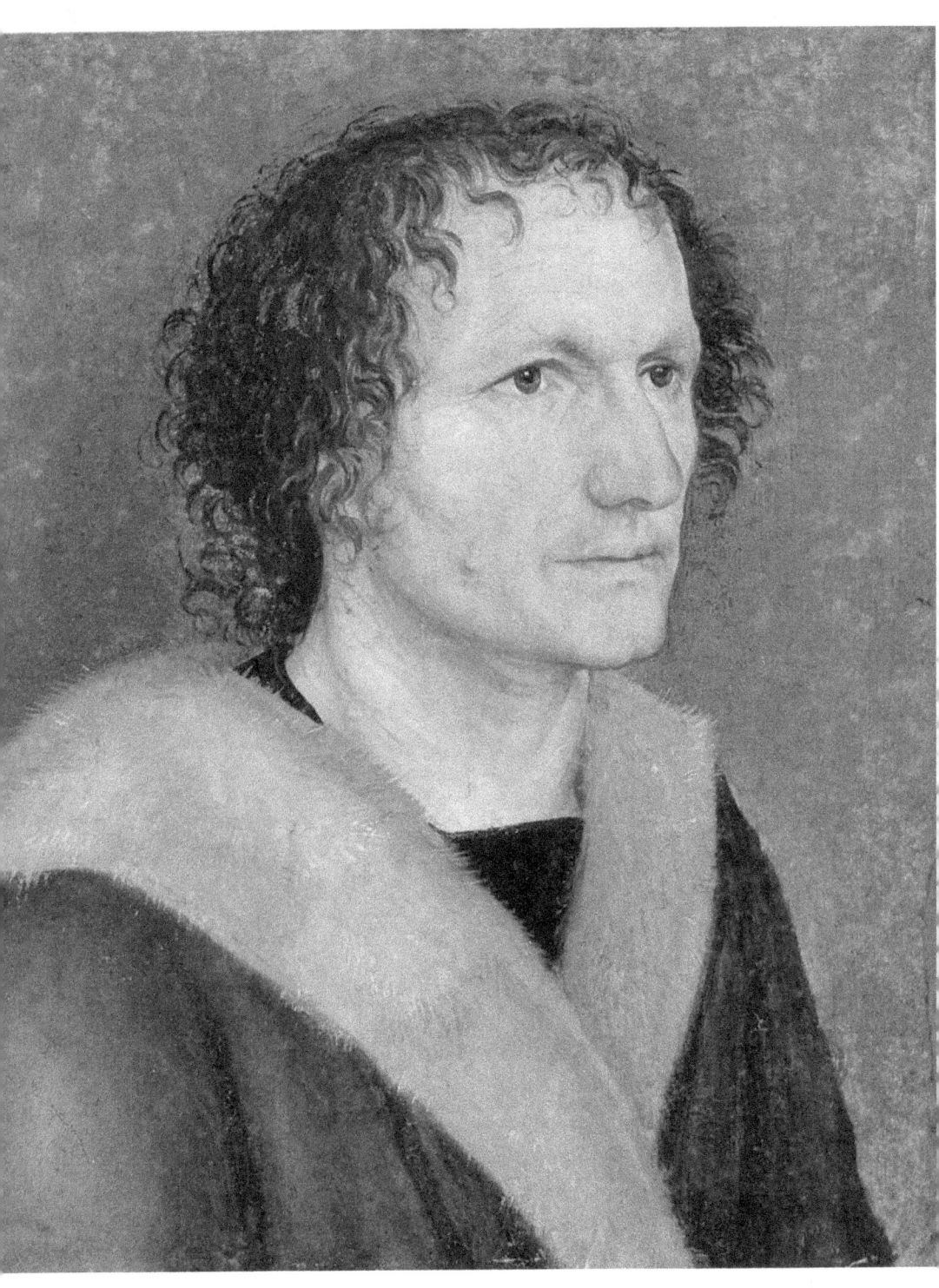

Albrecht Dürer, Männliches Porträt vor grünem Grund, 1497

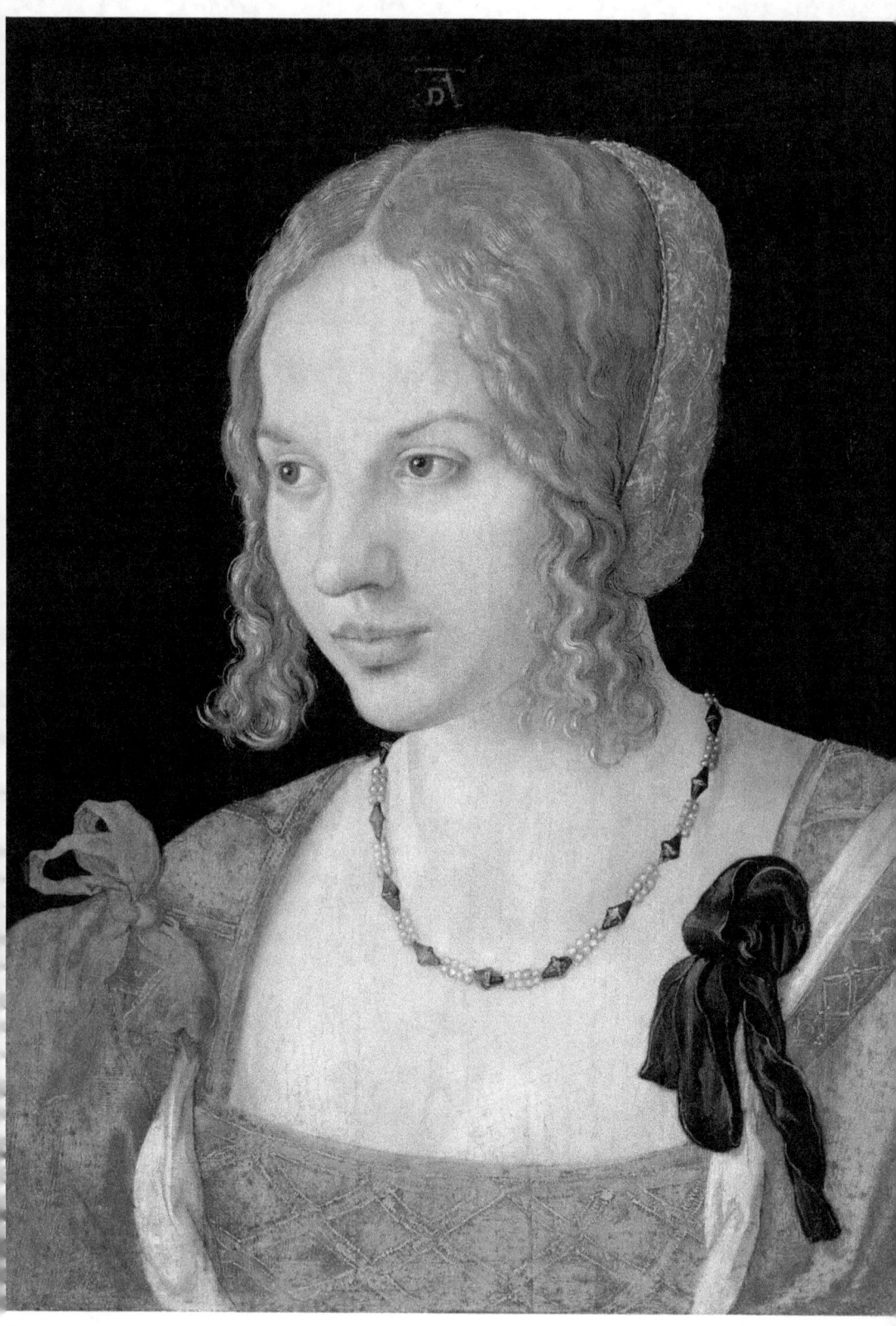

Albrecht Dürer, Portrait of a Young Woman, 1505, Vienna

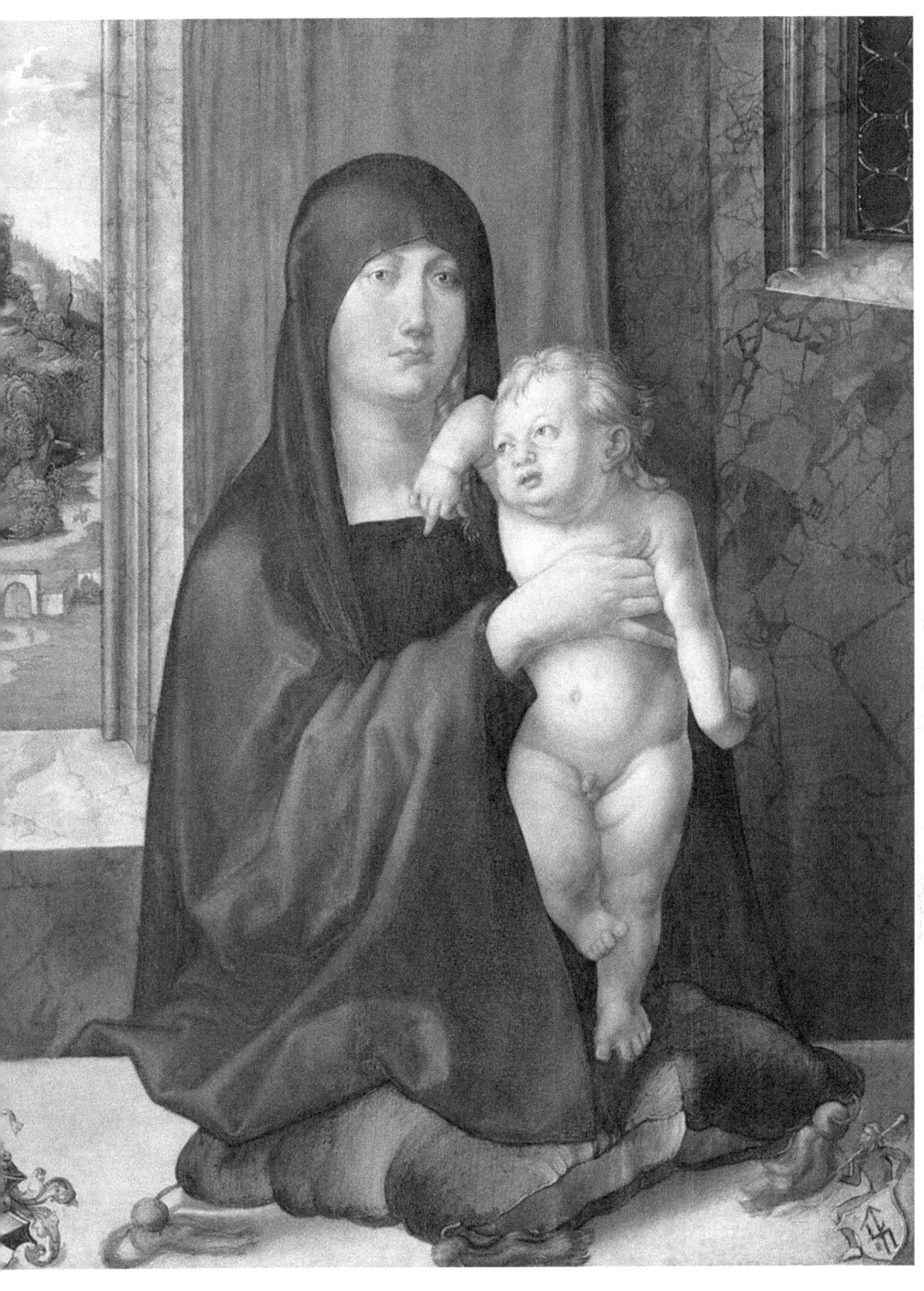

Albrecht Dürer, Madonna Haller, 1499, Washington, DC

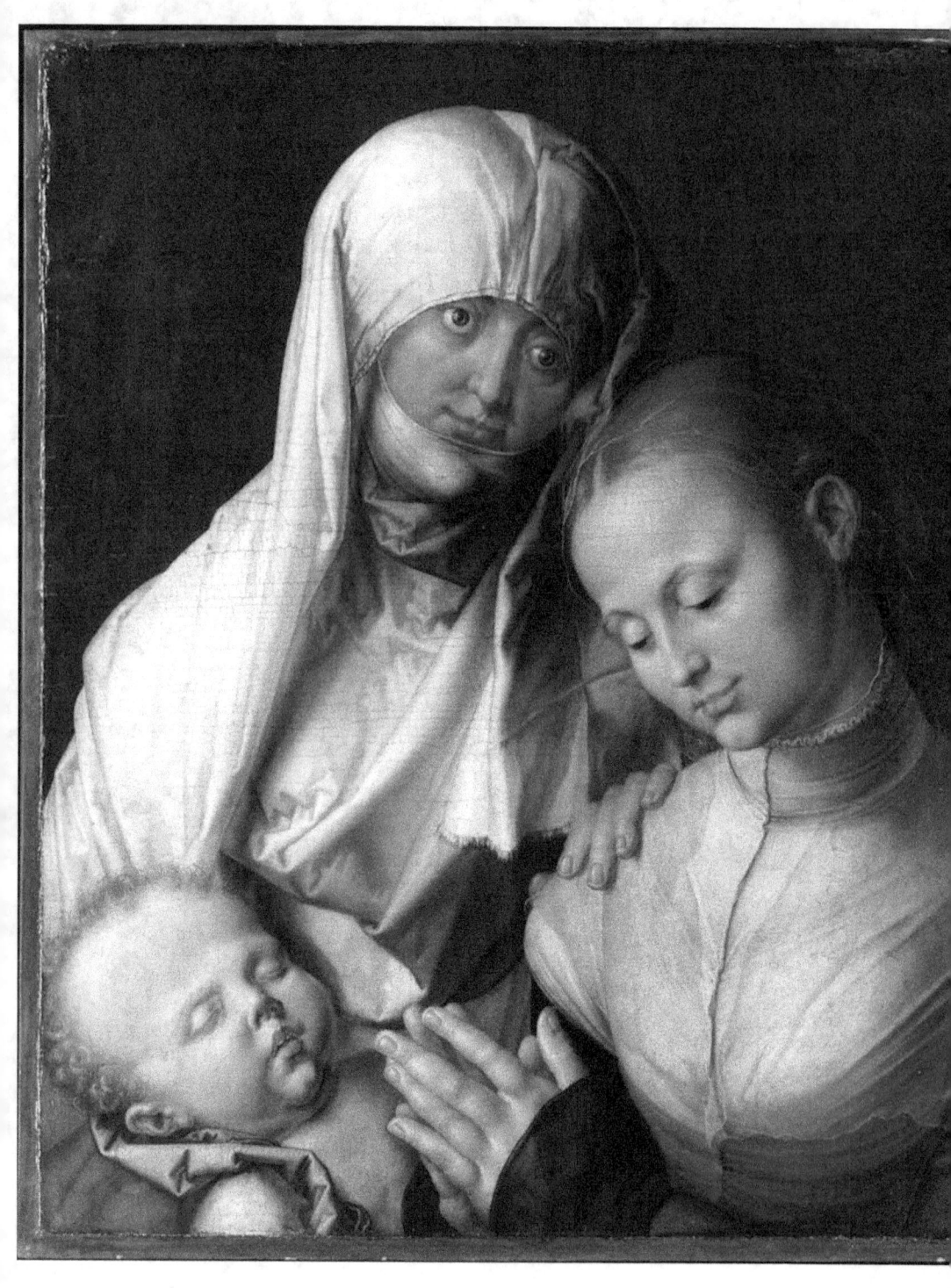

Albrecht Dürer, Virgin and Child, 1518,
Metropolitan Museum of Art, New York City

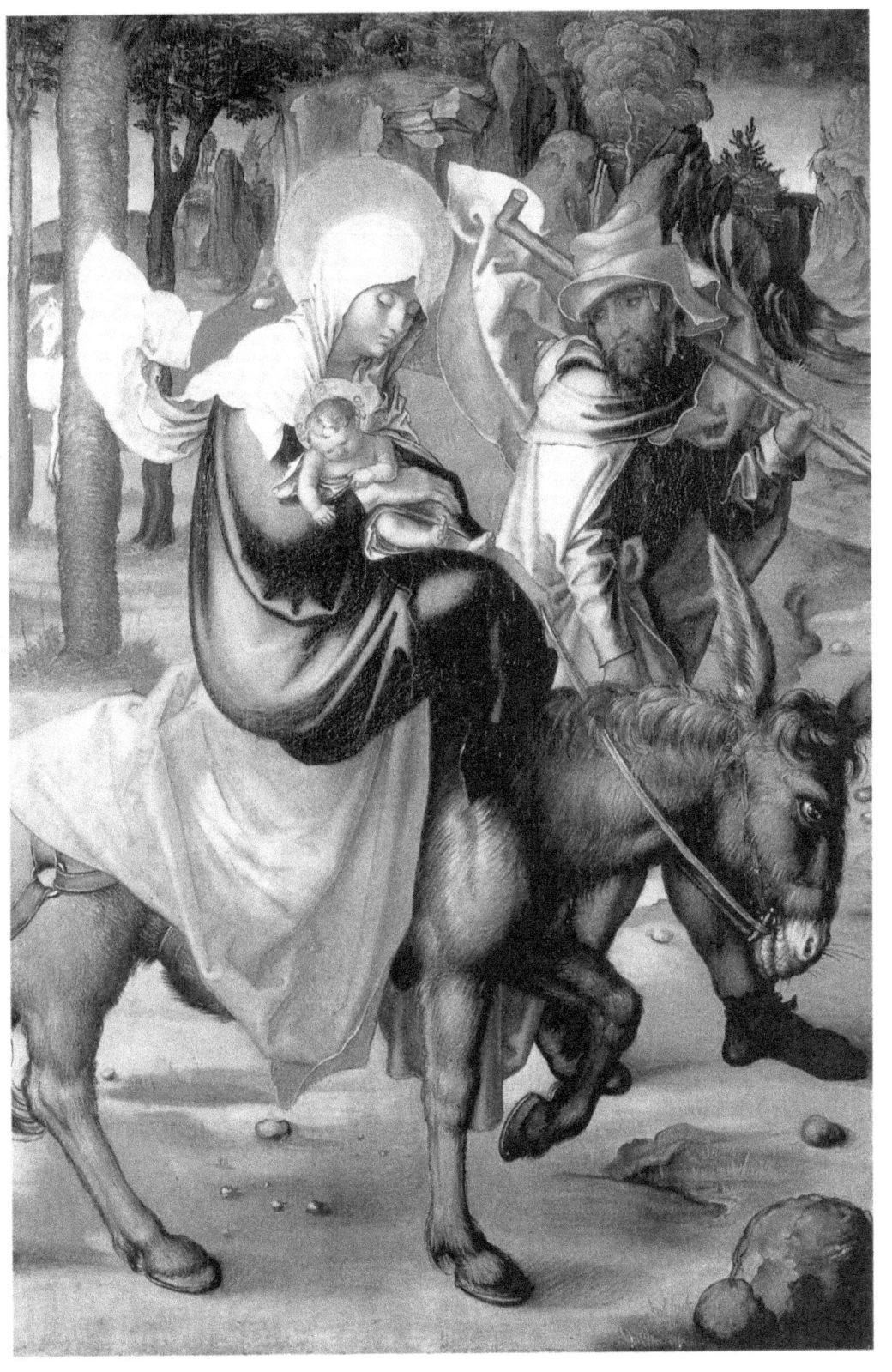

Albrecht Dürer, The Seven Sorrows of Mary, Munich

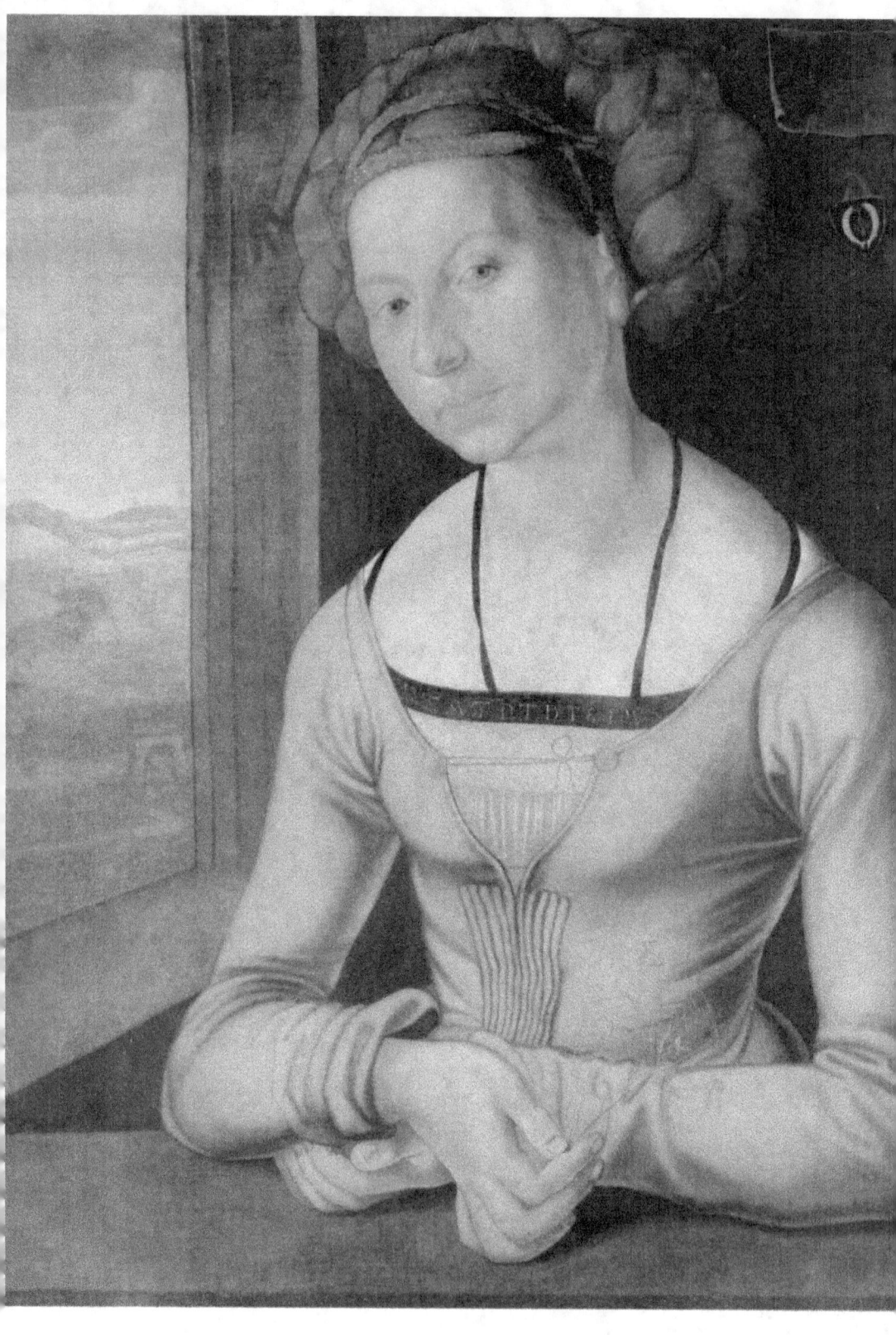

Albrecht Dürer, Young Woman With Braided Hair, 1497, Berlin

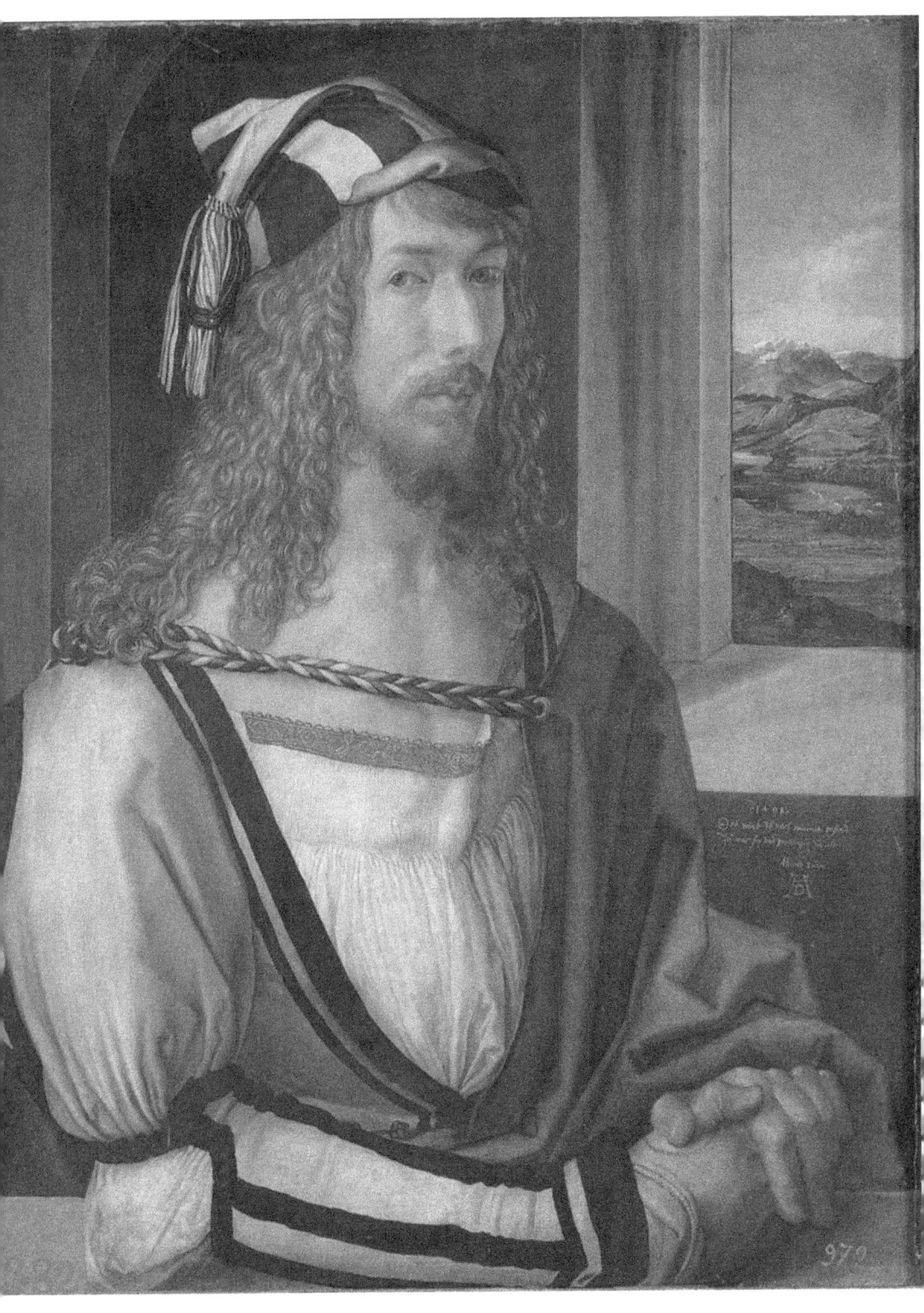

Albrecht Dürer, Self-Portrait, 1498, Prado, Madrid

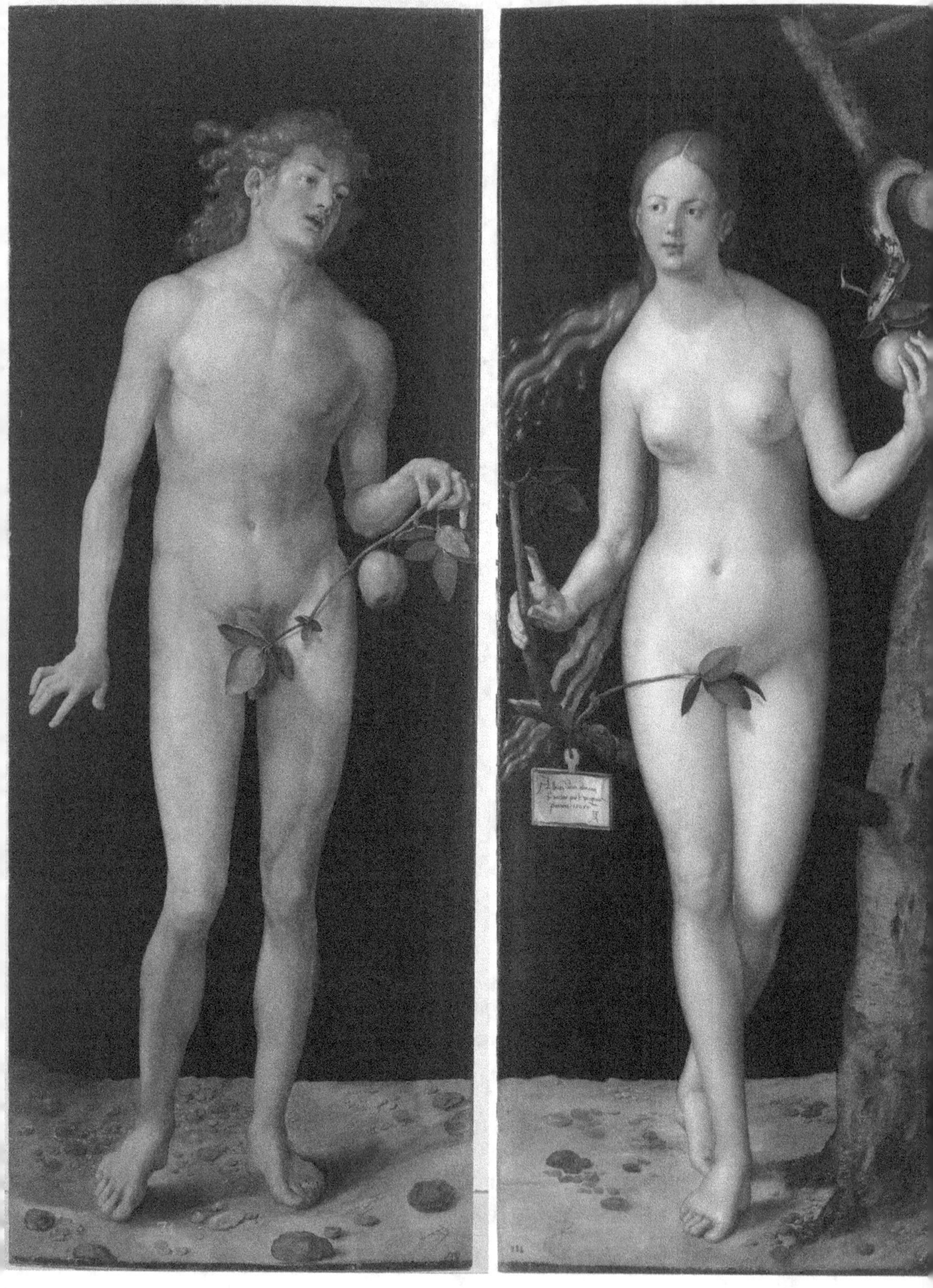

Albrecht Dürer, Adam and Eve, 1507, Prado, Madrid

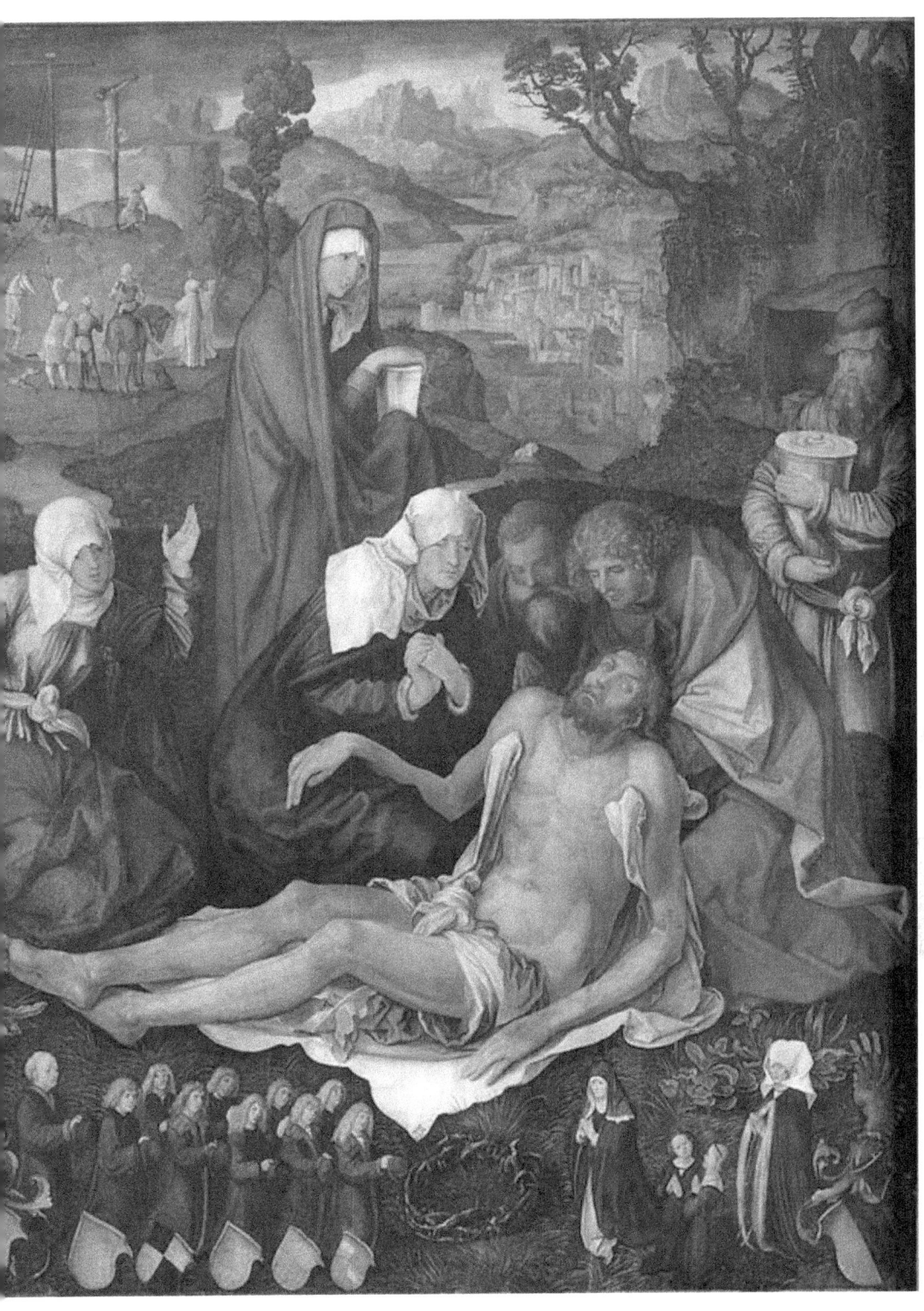

Albrecht Dürer, Lamentation, 1500, Nuremberg

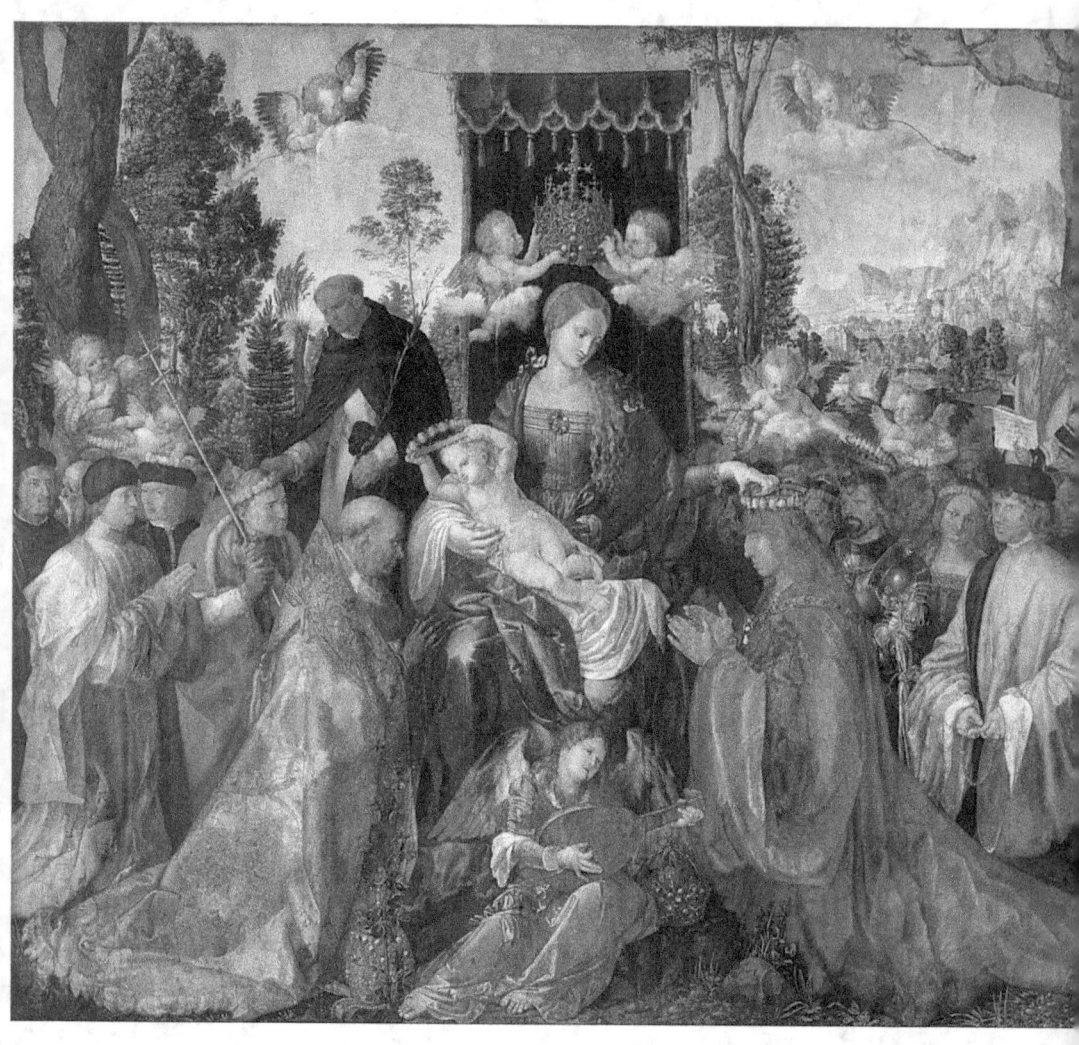

Albrecht Dürer, The Feast of Rose Garlands, 1506, Prague

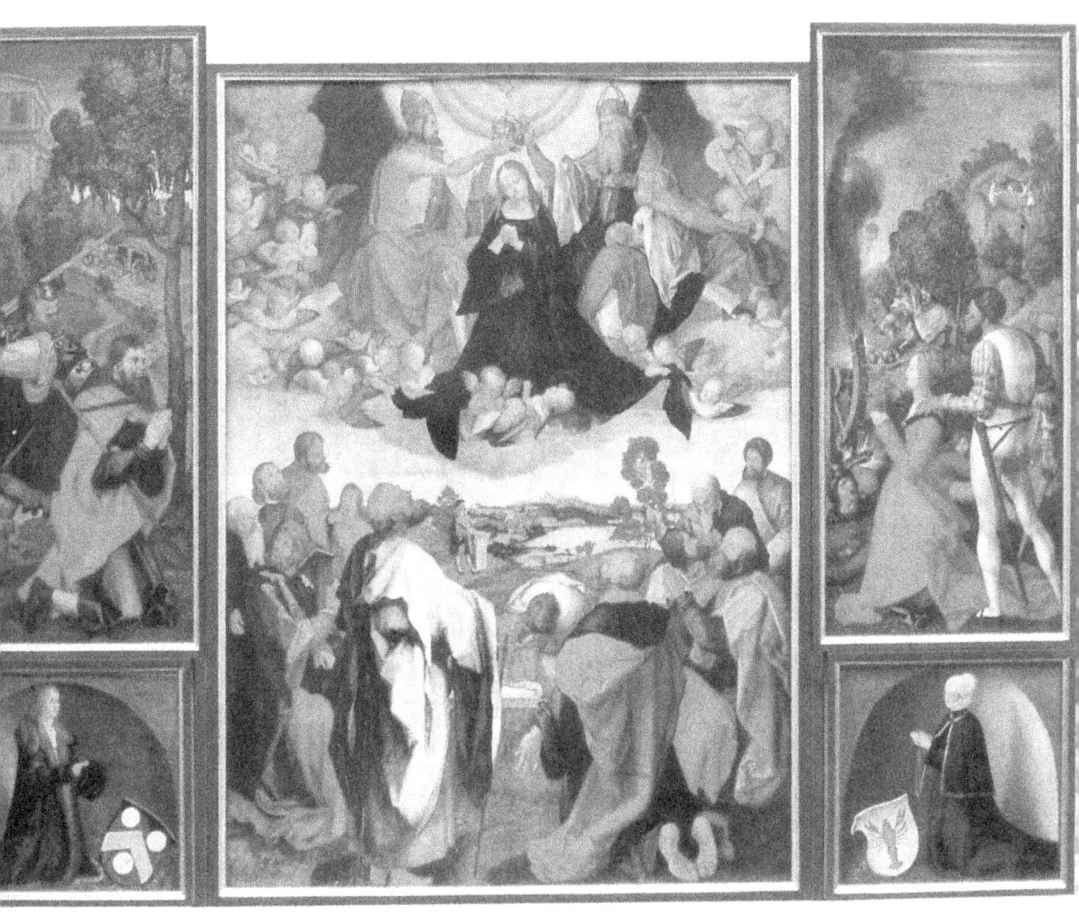

Albrecht Dürer, Heller Altarpiece, 1506-08, Frankfurt

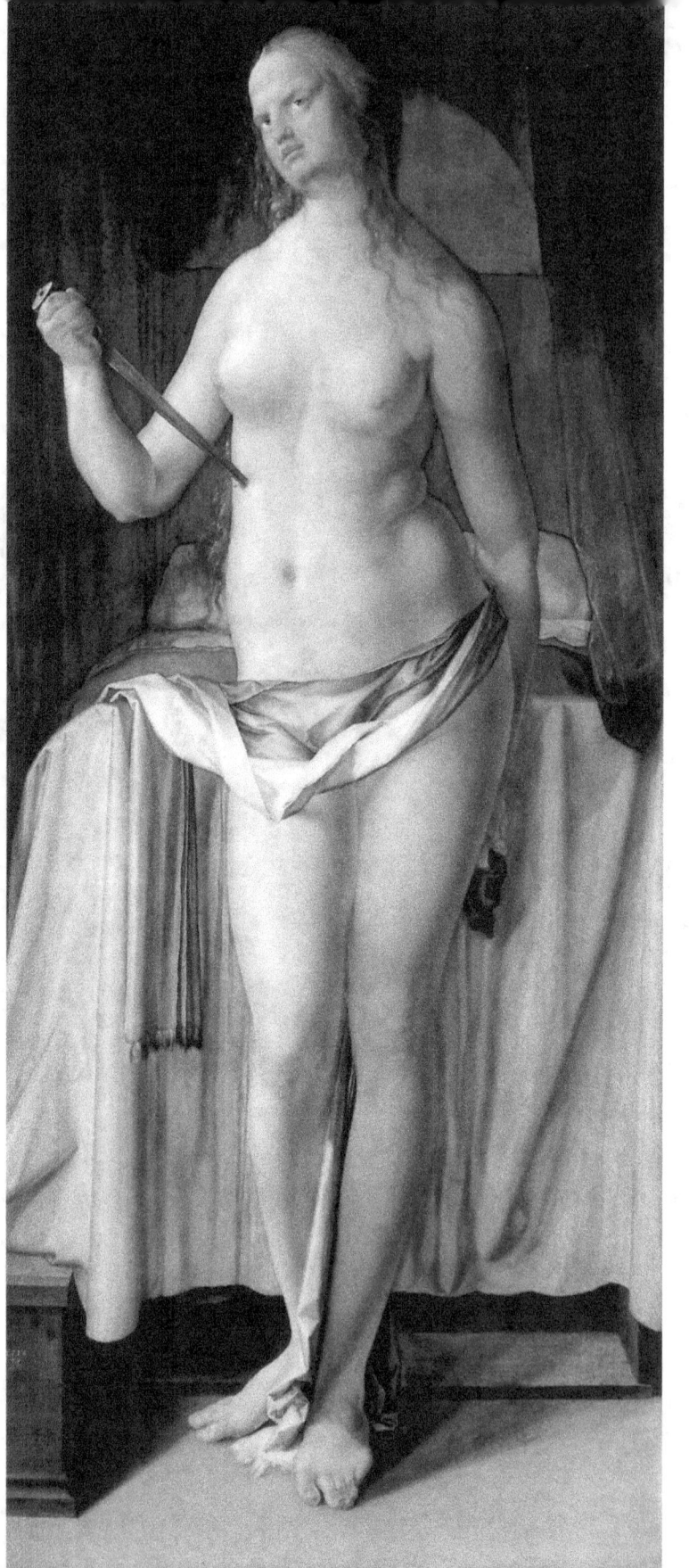

Albrecht Dürer,
Lucrezia, 1518,
Munich

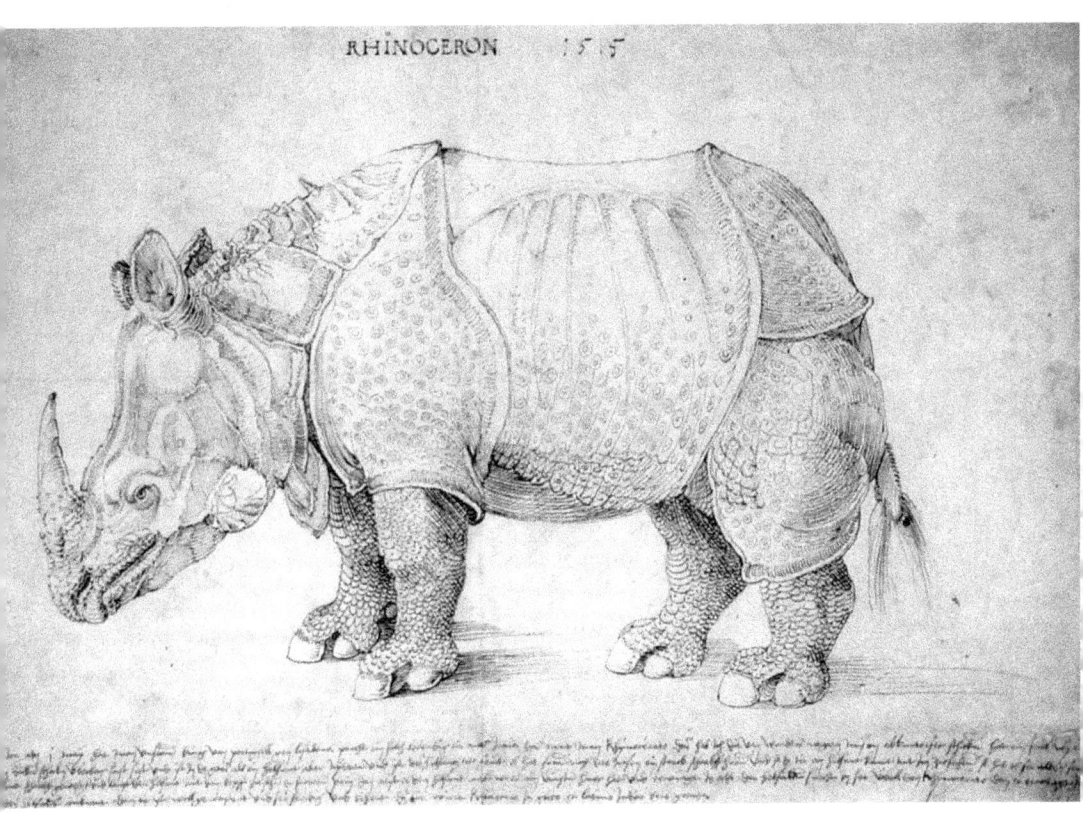

Albrecht Dürer, Rhinoceros

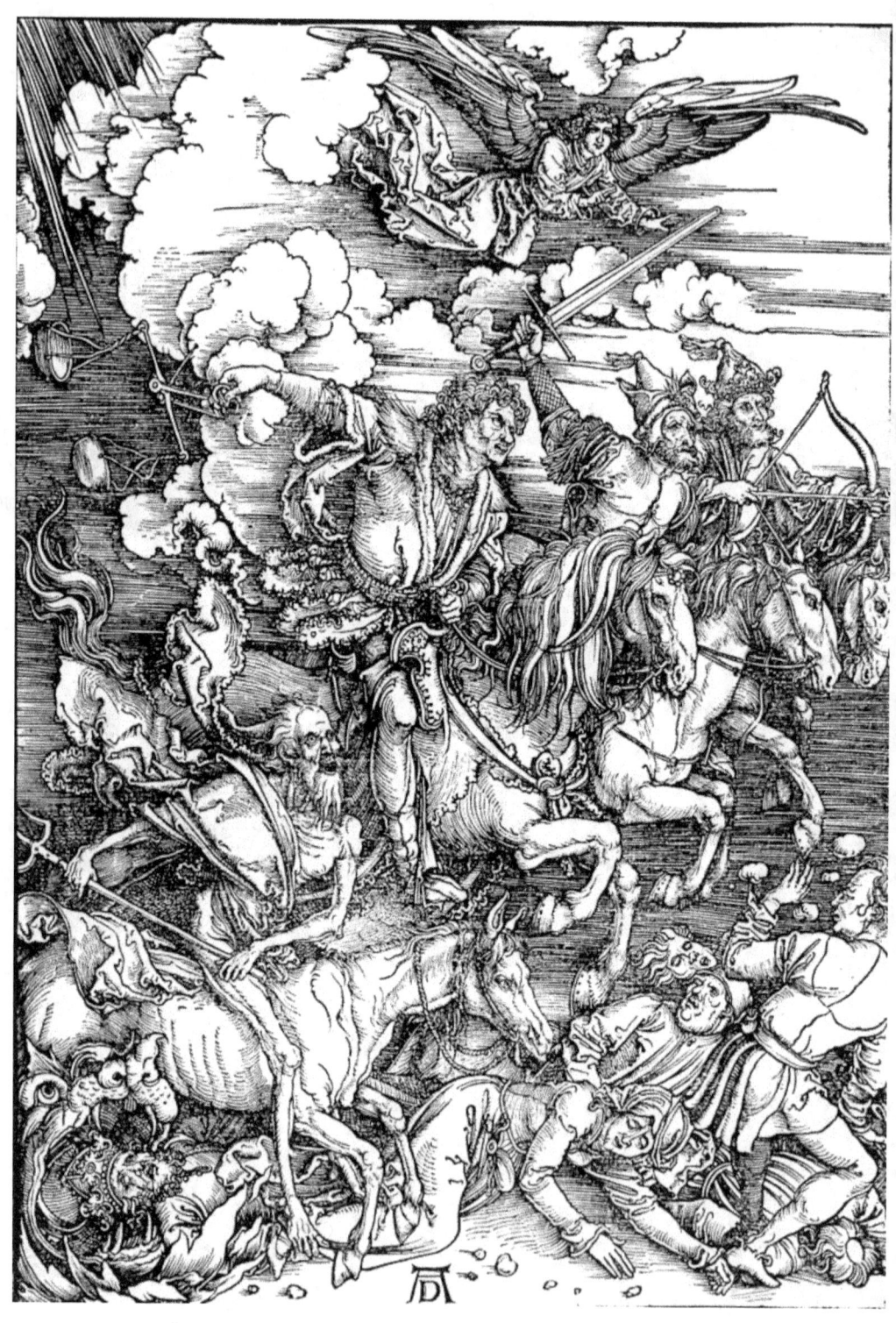

Albrecht Dürer, The Four Horseman of the Apocalypse, 1498

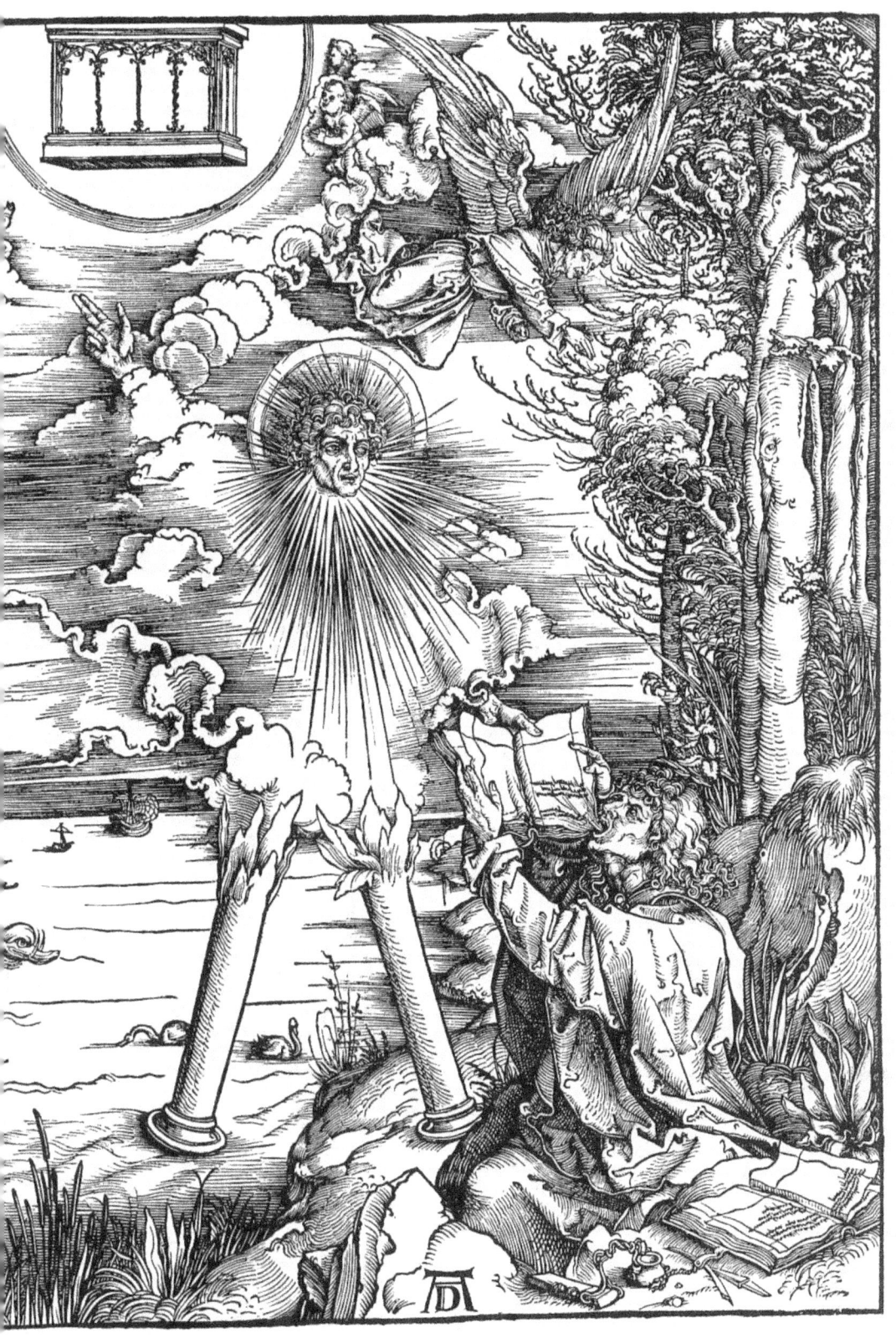

Albrecht Dürer, The Revelation of St John, 1498

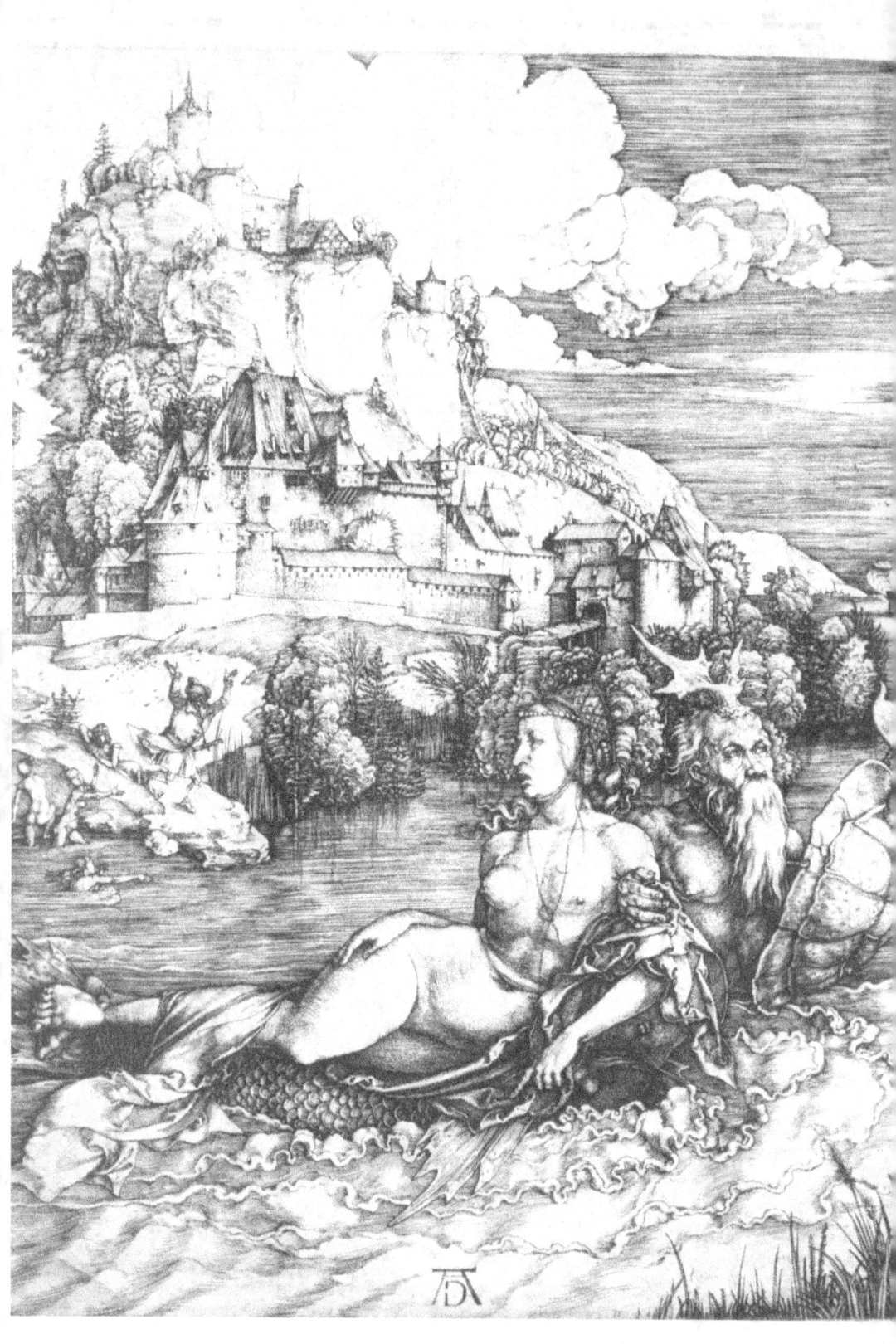

Albrecht Dürer, Sea Monster, 1498

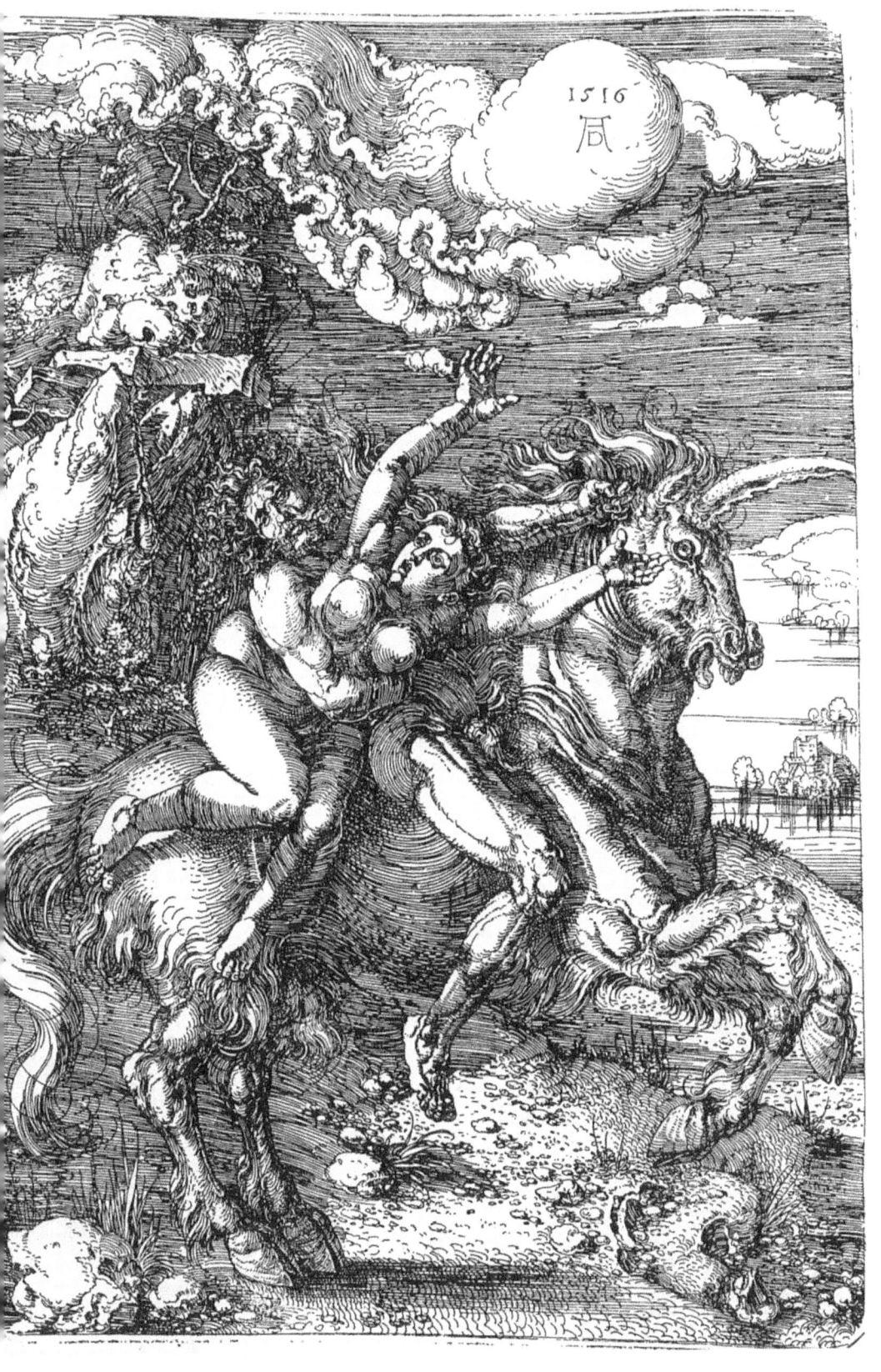

Albrecht Dürer, Abduction of the Unicorn, 1516,
Metropolitan Museum of Art, New York City

NOTES ON WORKS

PORTRAIT OF A WOMAN
(From the Oil-painting in the Berlin Museum)

This beautiful portrait represents, artistically, the zenith of Dürer's art. It shows Venetian influence so strongly, and is painted with so much serenity of manner, that one is almost inclined to doubt its ascription.

PORTRAIT OF THE ARTIST
(From the Oil-painting in the Alte Pinakothek, Munich)

This picture bears the date 1500 and a Latin inscription, "I, Albert Dürer, of Nuremberg, painted my own portrait here in the proper colours, at the age of twenty-eight."

According to Thausing, this picture had a curious fate. The panel on which it was painted was sawn in two by an engraver to whom it was lent, and who affixed the back to his own poor copy of the picture – thus using the seal of the Nuremberg magistrates, which was placed upon it, to authenticate his copy as a genuine work of the master.

PORTRAIT OF THE PAINTER'S FATHER
(From the Oil-painting in the National Gallery. Painted in 1497)

An interesting picture, which has unfortunately suffered by retouching. It is the only portrait by Dürer the nation possesses. Other works of his may be seen at South Kensington and at Hampton Court.

PORTRAIT OF OSWALT KREL
(From the Oil-painting in the Alte Pinakothek, Munich. Painted in 1499)

A striking portrait; somewhat cramped in expression, but full of interest. The trees in the background stamp it at once as a work of German origin. Dürer's attempt to portray more than the flesh is particularly noticeable here, because not quite successful.

THE MADONNA WITH THE SISKIN
(From the Oil-painting in the Berlin Museum. Painted about 1506)

Although this picture shows that it was painted under Venetian influence, it betrays the unrest of Dürer's mind, which makes nearly all his work pleasanter to look *into* than to look *at*. Dürer's works generally should be *read*.

SS. JOHN AND PETER

(From an Oil-painting in the Alte Pinakothek, Munich. Finished in 1526)

This, with the "SS. Paul and Mark," originally formed one picture, and was painted for the Council of his beloved city, Nuremberg, as a gift, two years before his death. Dürer had inscribed lengthy quotations from the Bible below the picture; these quotations, proving the militant fervour of his Protestant faith, were subsequently removed on that account. Dürer's works were always more than works of *Art*.

On the following pages are illustrations of some of the contemporaries of Dürer.

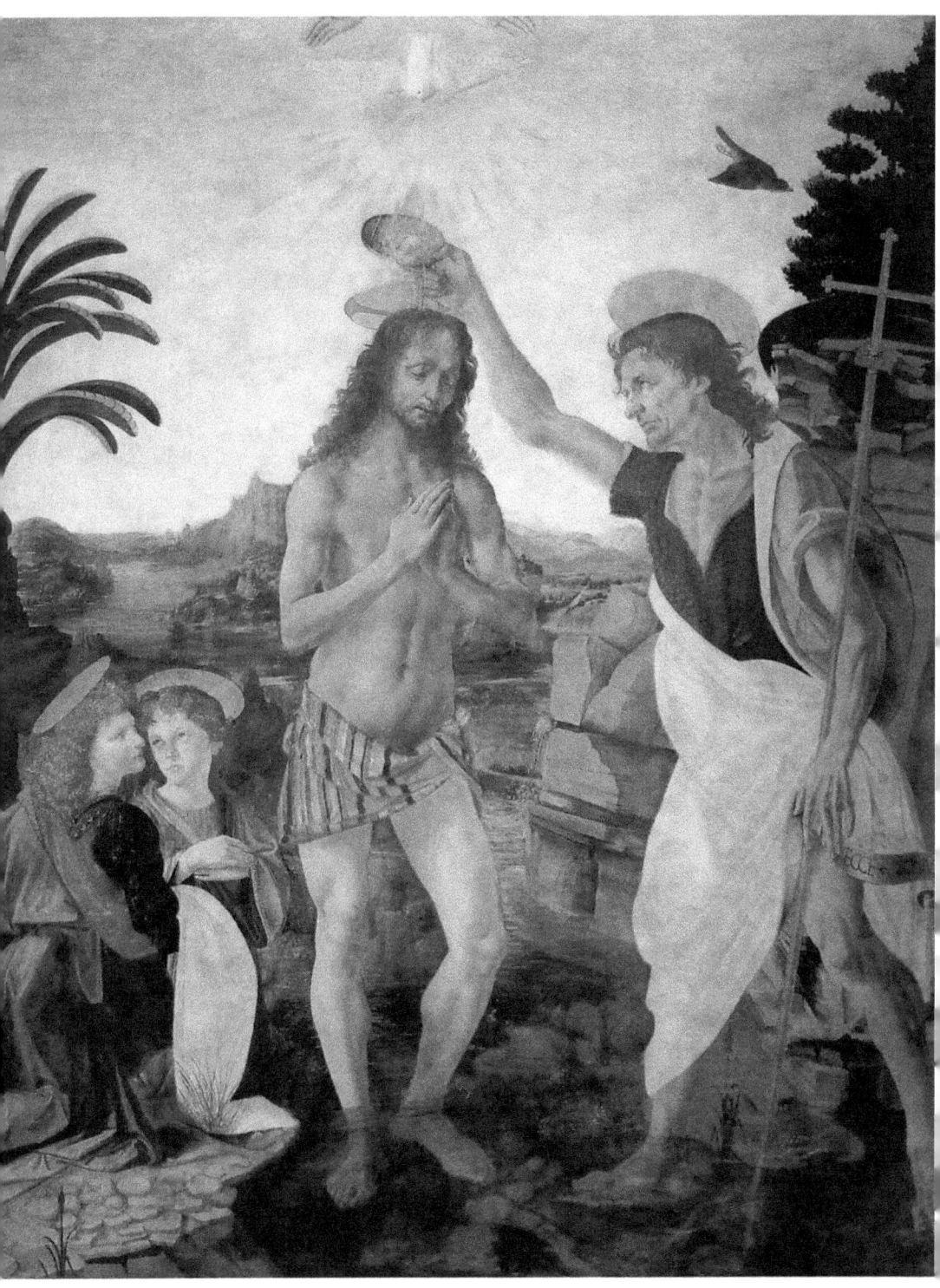

Andrea del Verrocchio, The Baptism of Christ

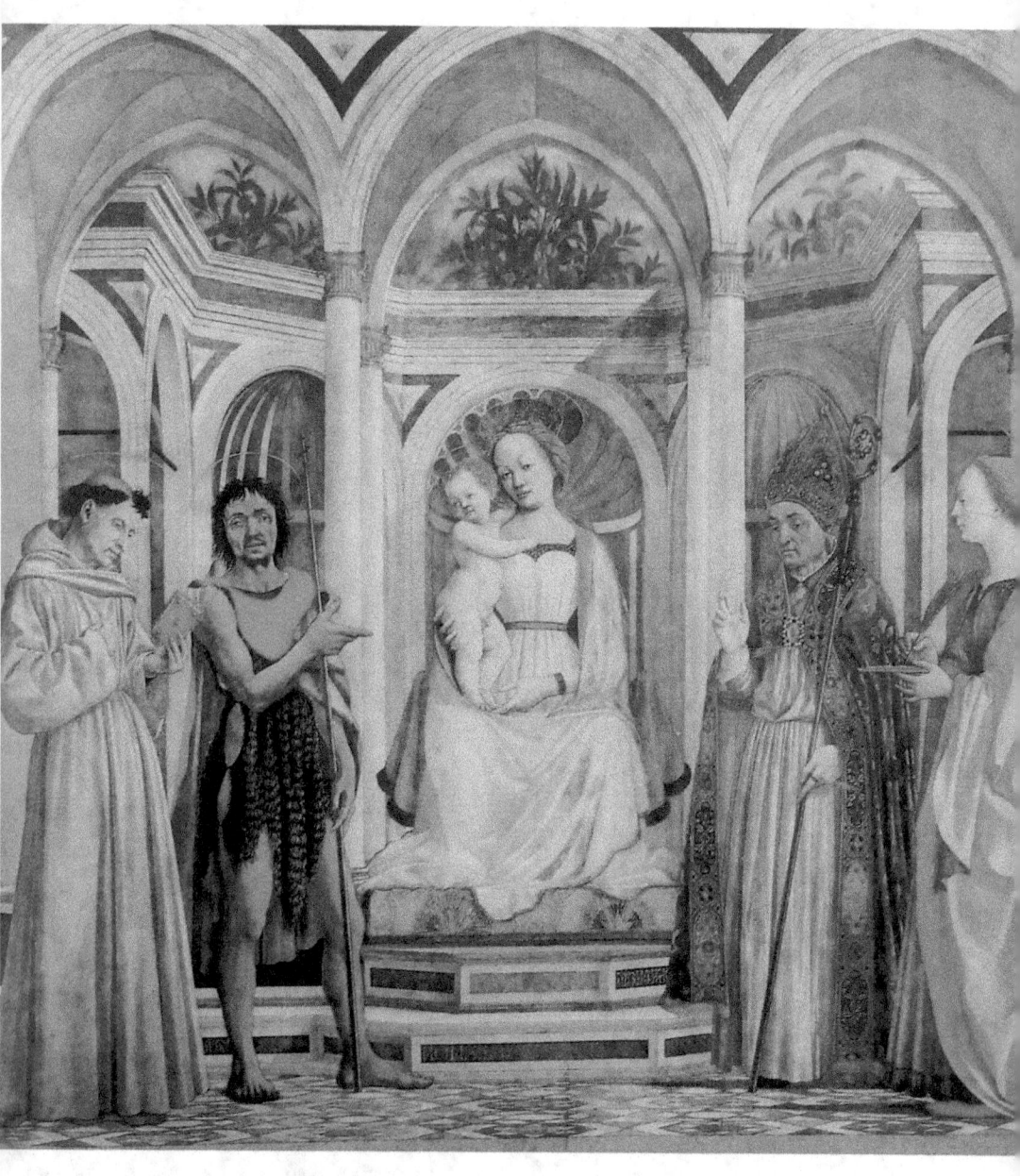

Domenico Veneziano, Madonna and Child With Saints, 1445, Uffizi Gallery

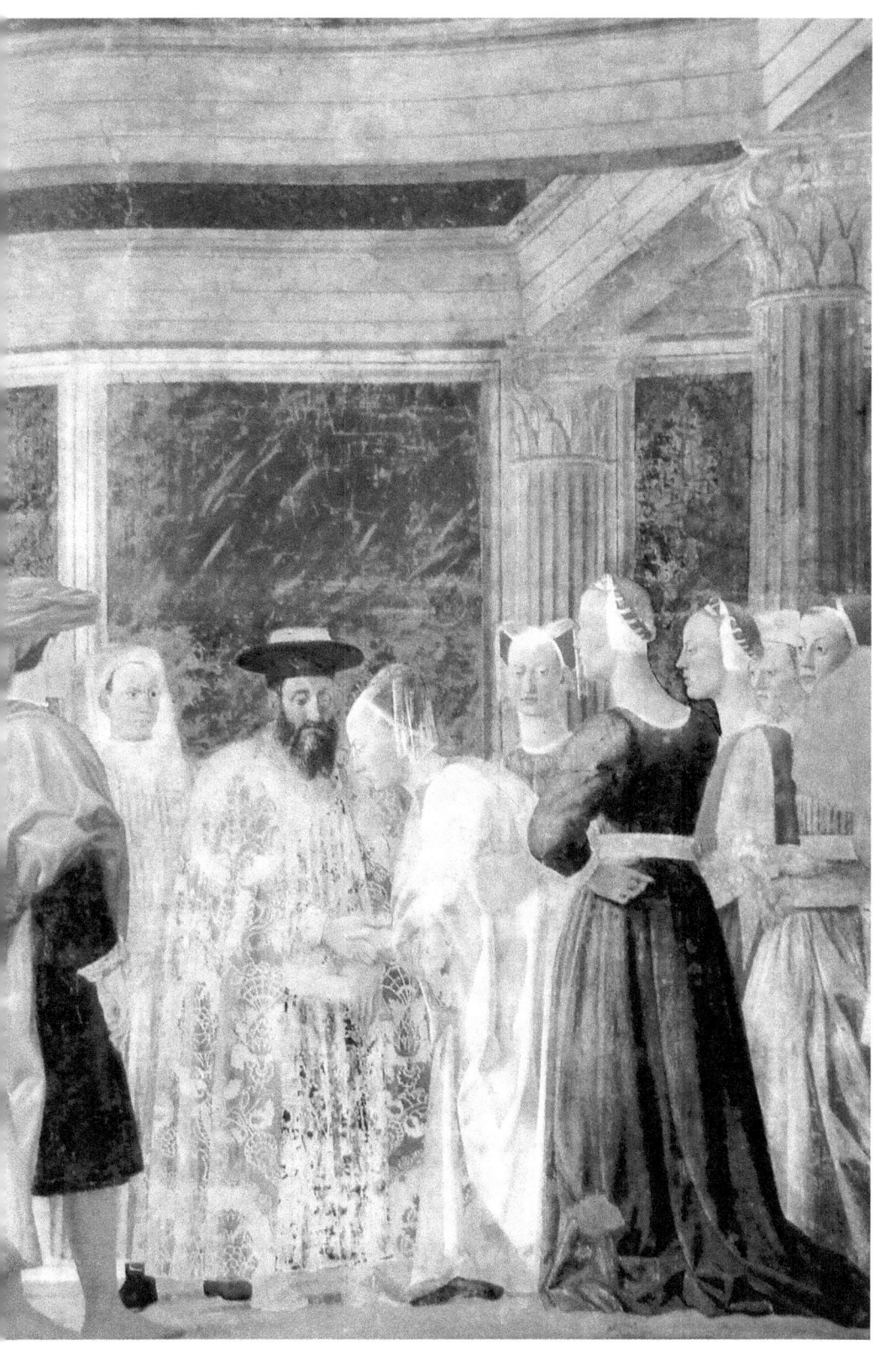

Piero della Francesca, frescoes, Arezzo

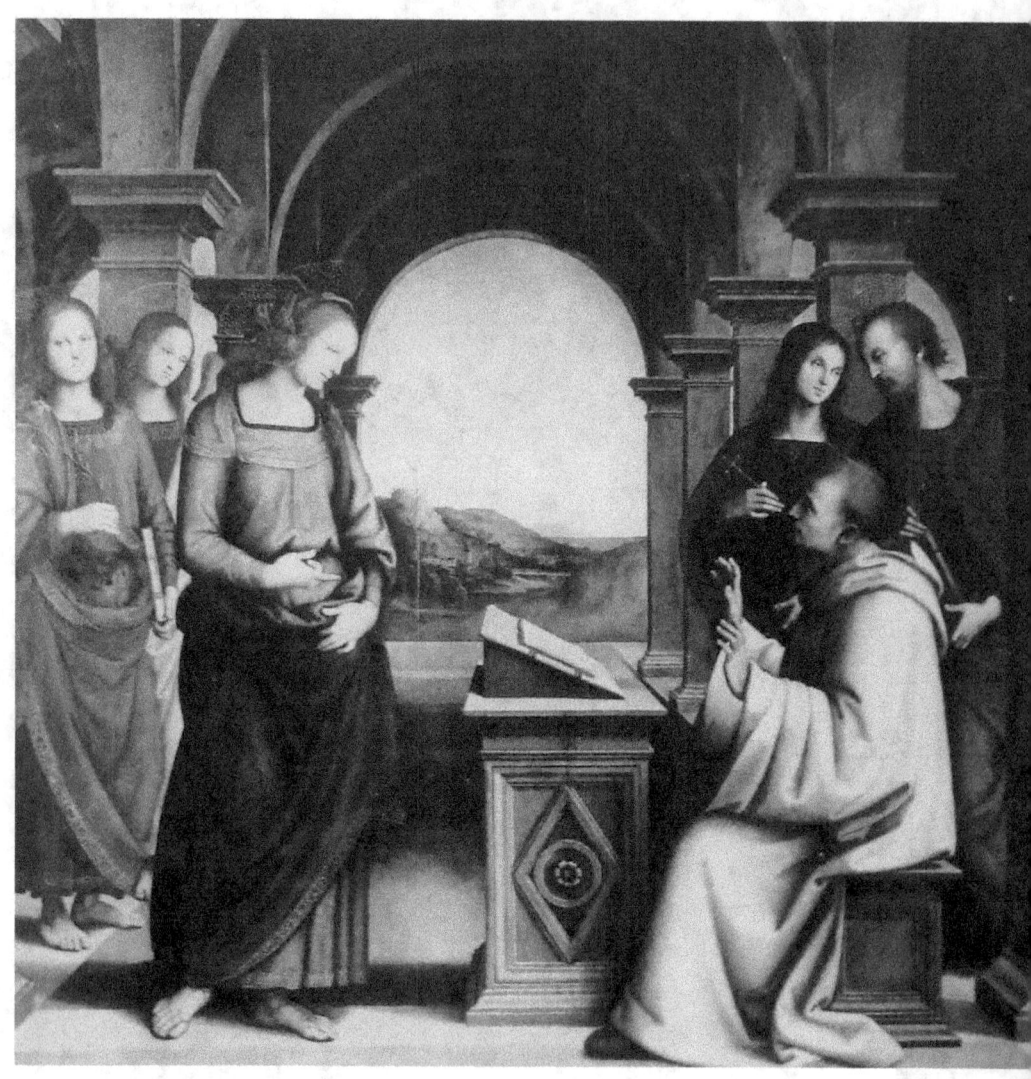

Perugino, Vision of St Bernard, 1488

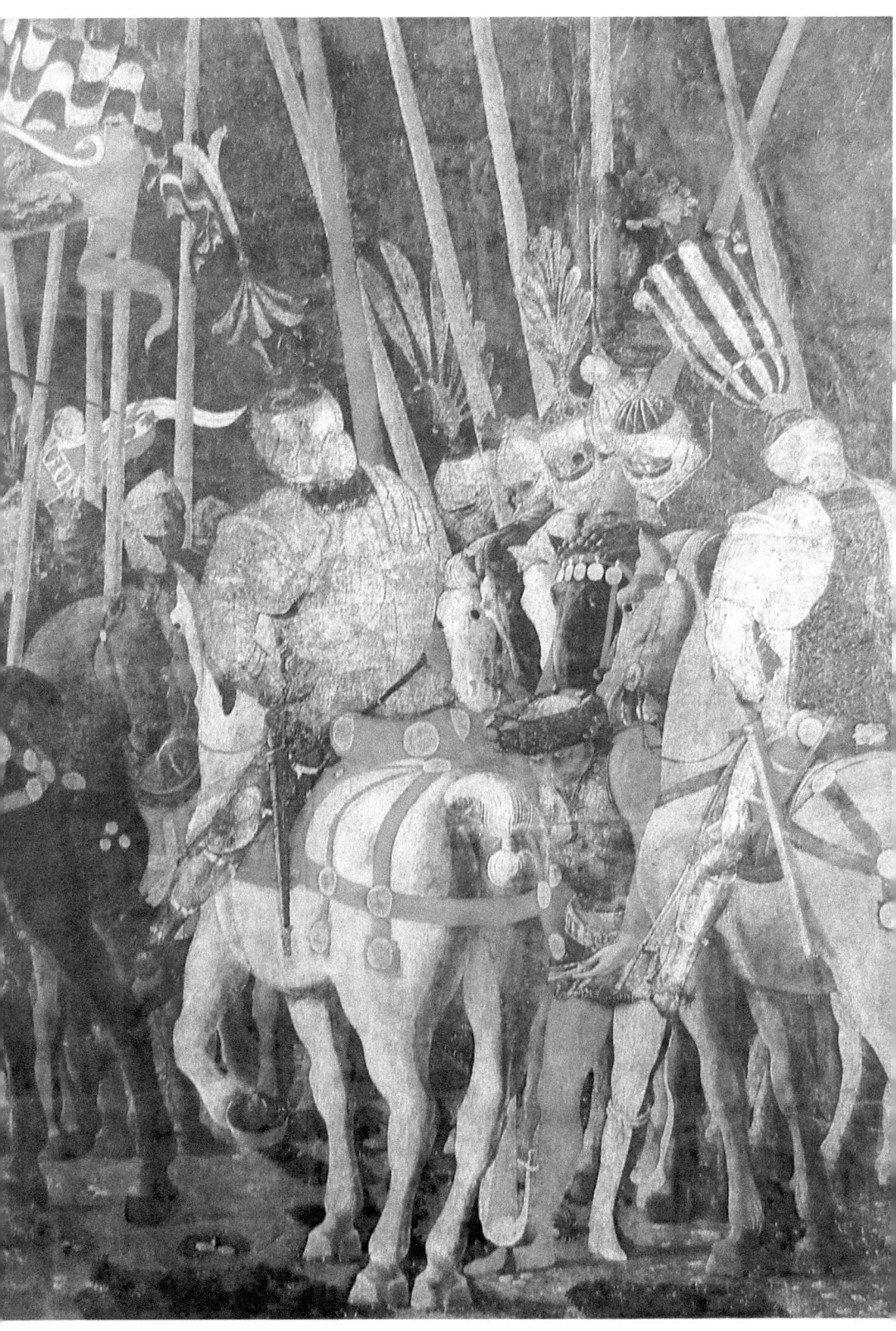

Paolo Uccello, The Battle of San Romano, Paris

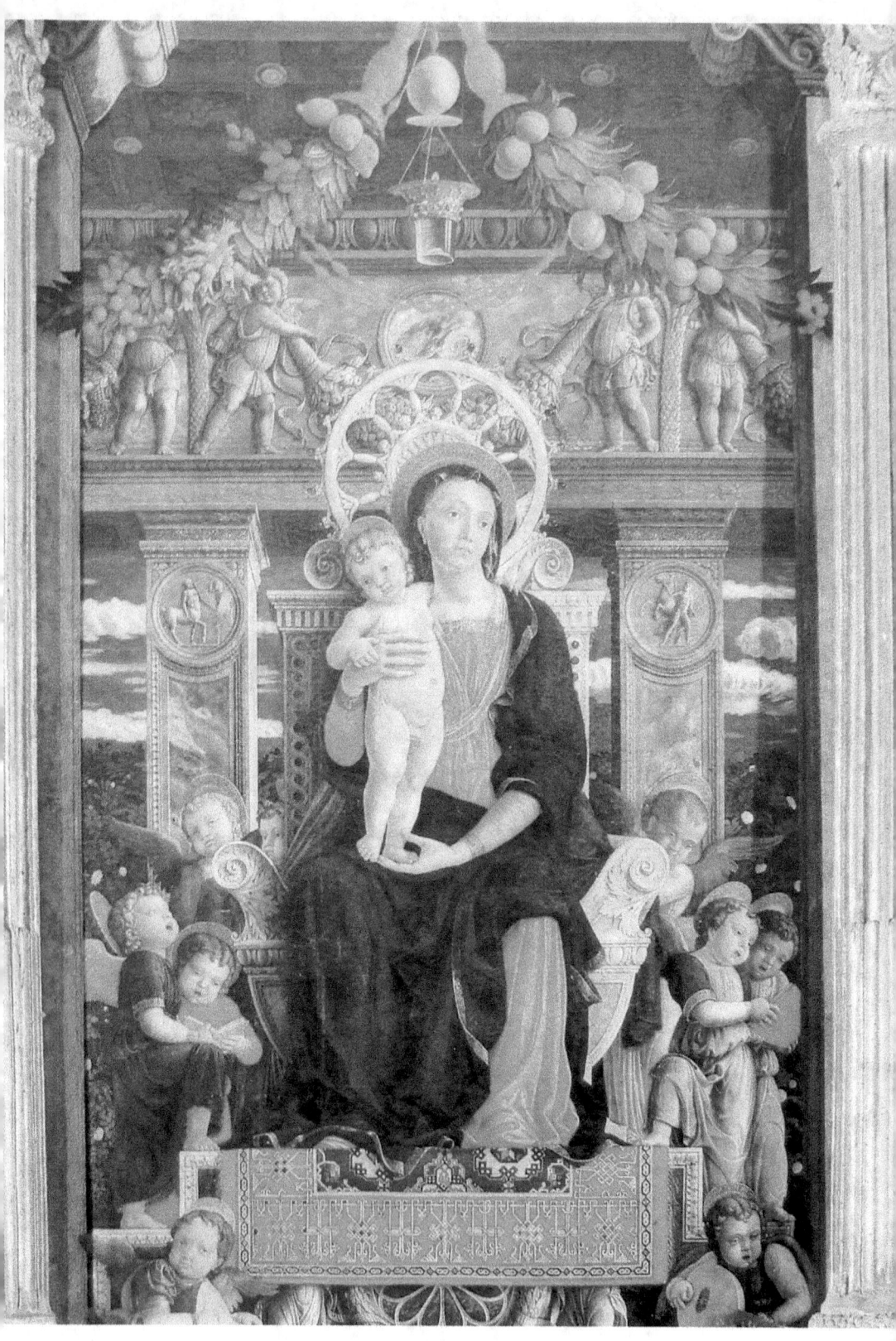

Andreas Mantegna, Madonna and Child Enthroned, 1457-60, Verona

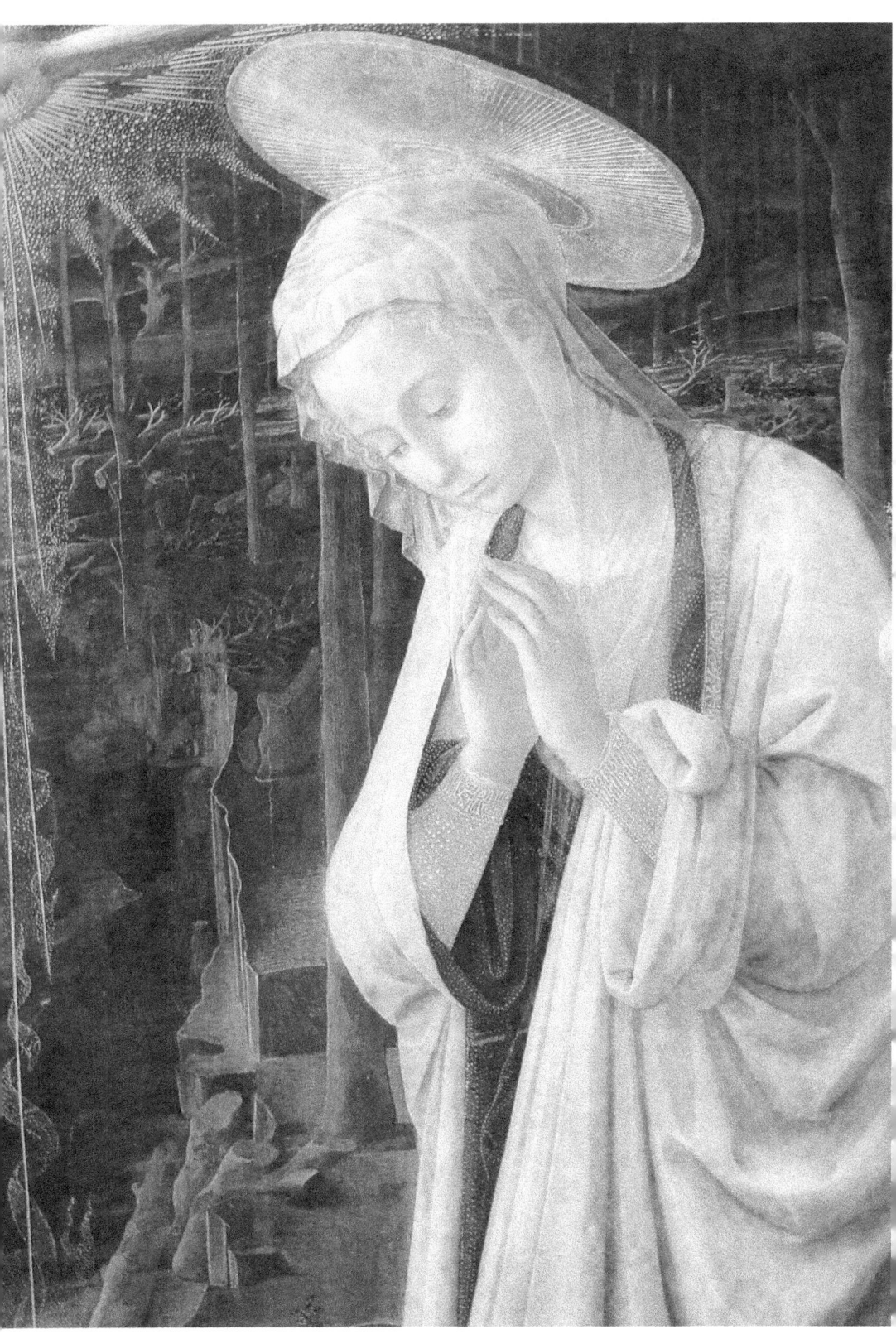

Fra Filippo Lippi, The Adoration of the Virgin, Berlin, detail

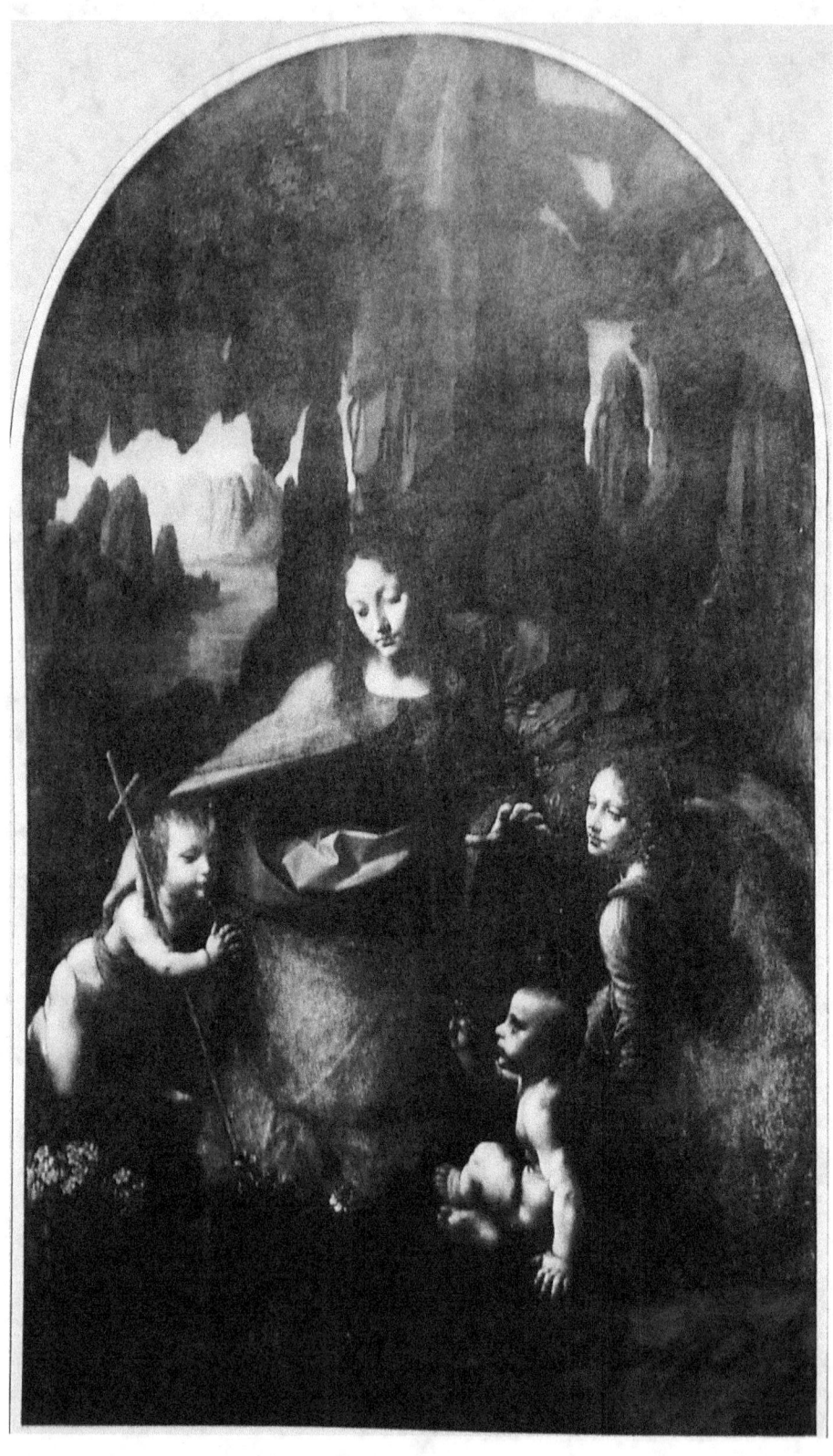

Leonardo da Vinci, The Madonna of the Rocks, London

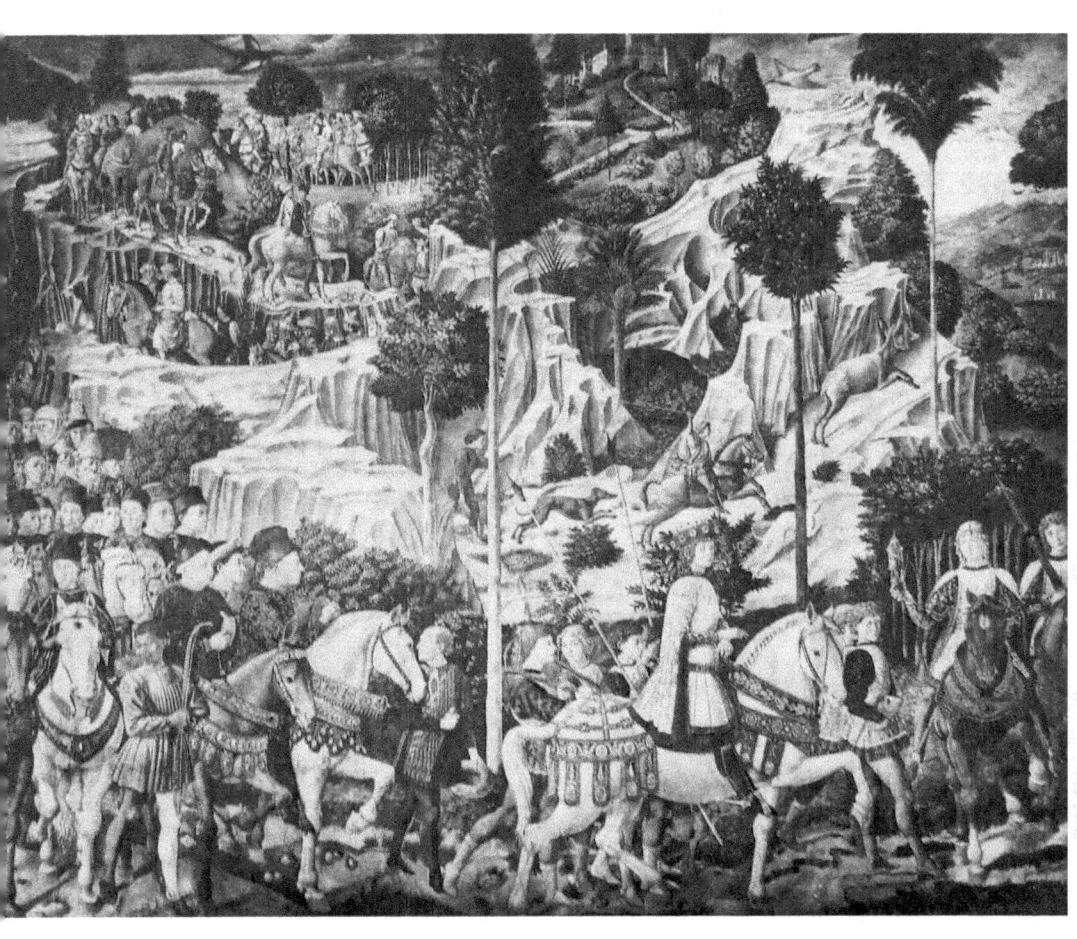

Benozzo Gozzoli, Journey of the Magi

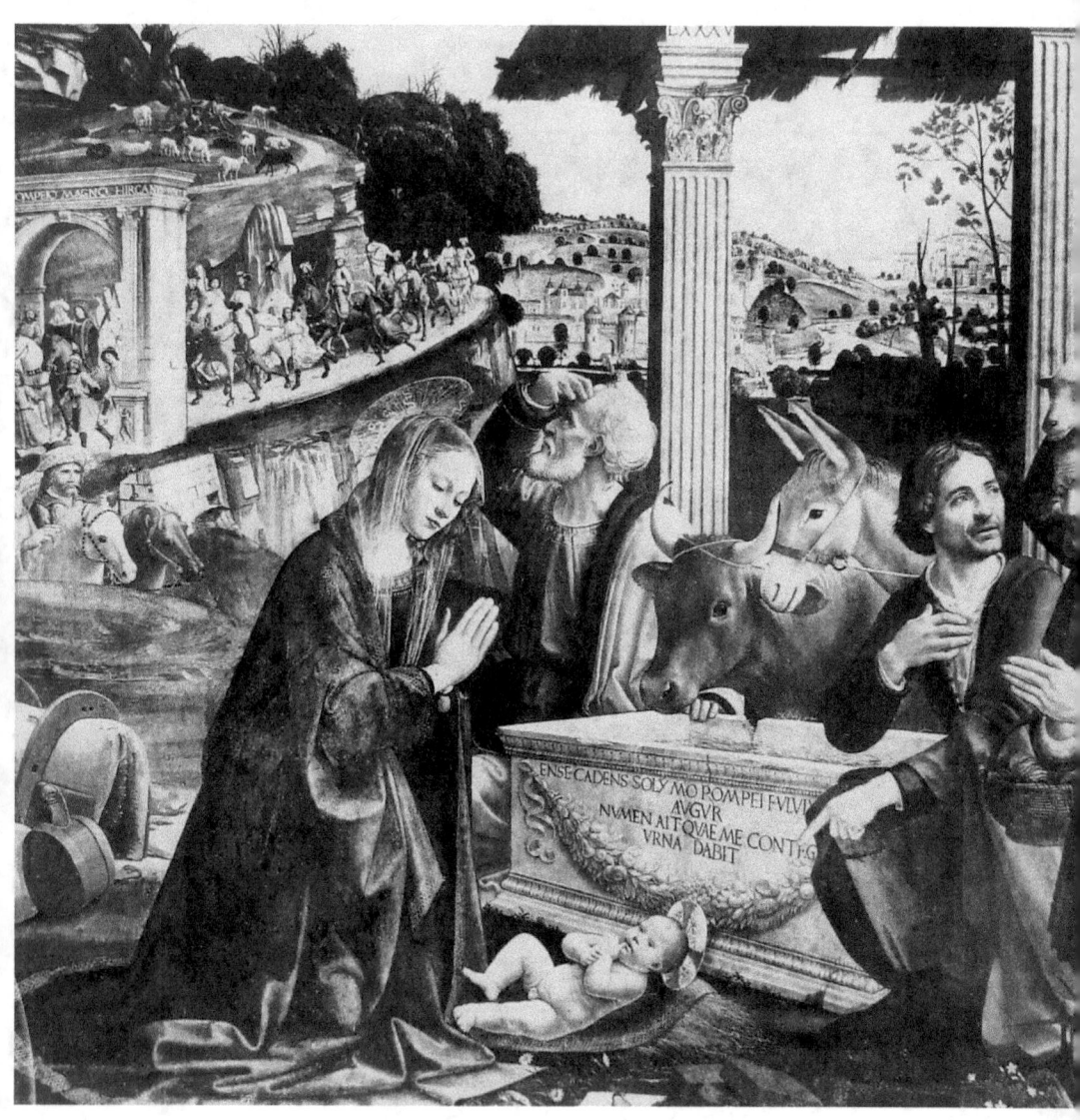

Domenico Ghirlandaio, Adoration of the Shepherds, 1485

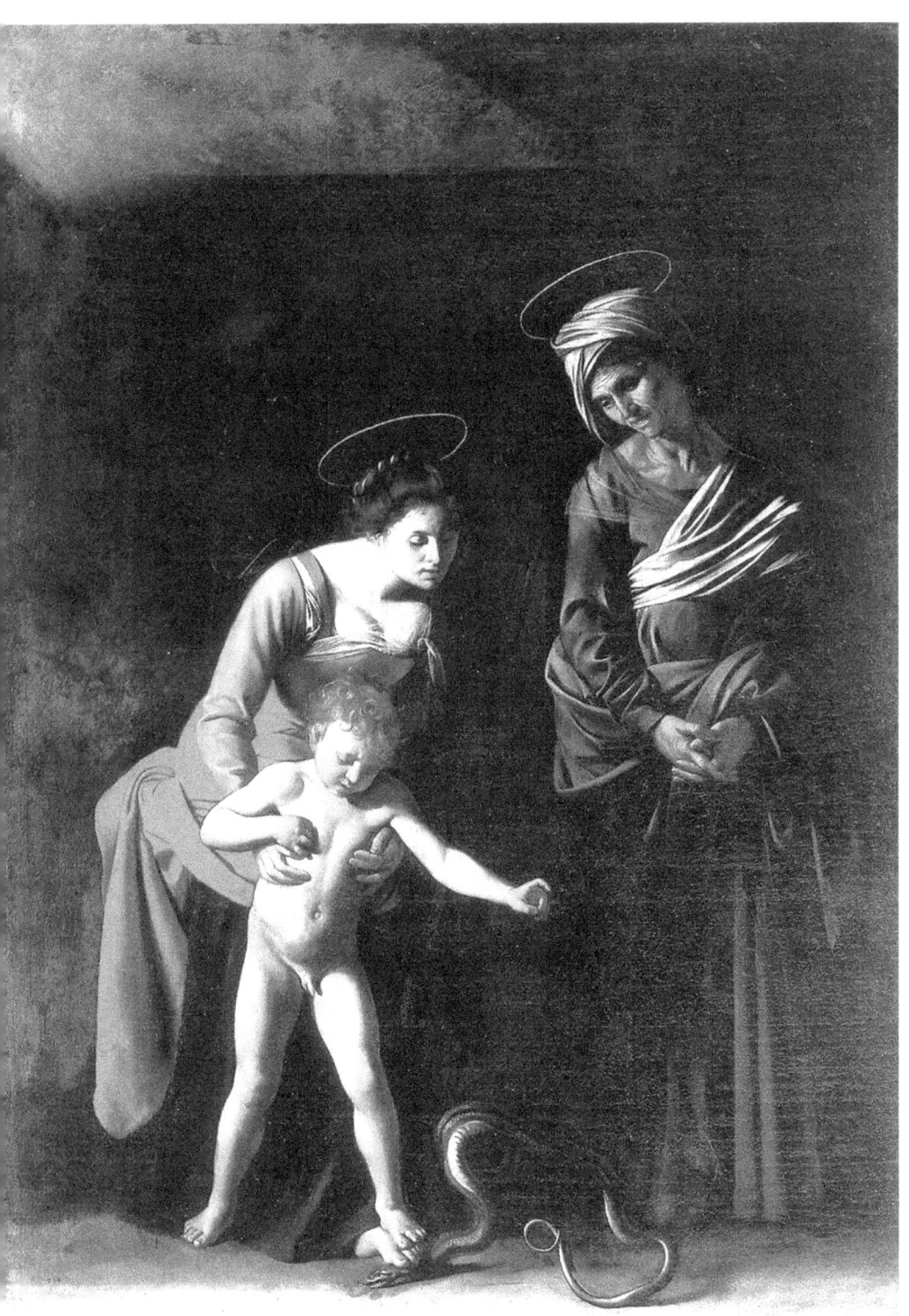

Michelangelo Merisi da Caravaggio, Madonna of the Palafrenieri,
1605-06, Galleria Borghese, Rome

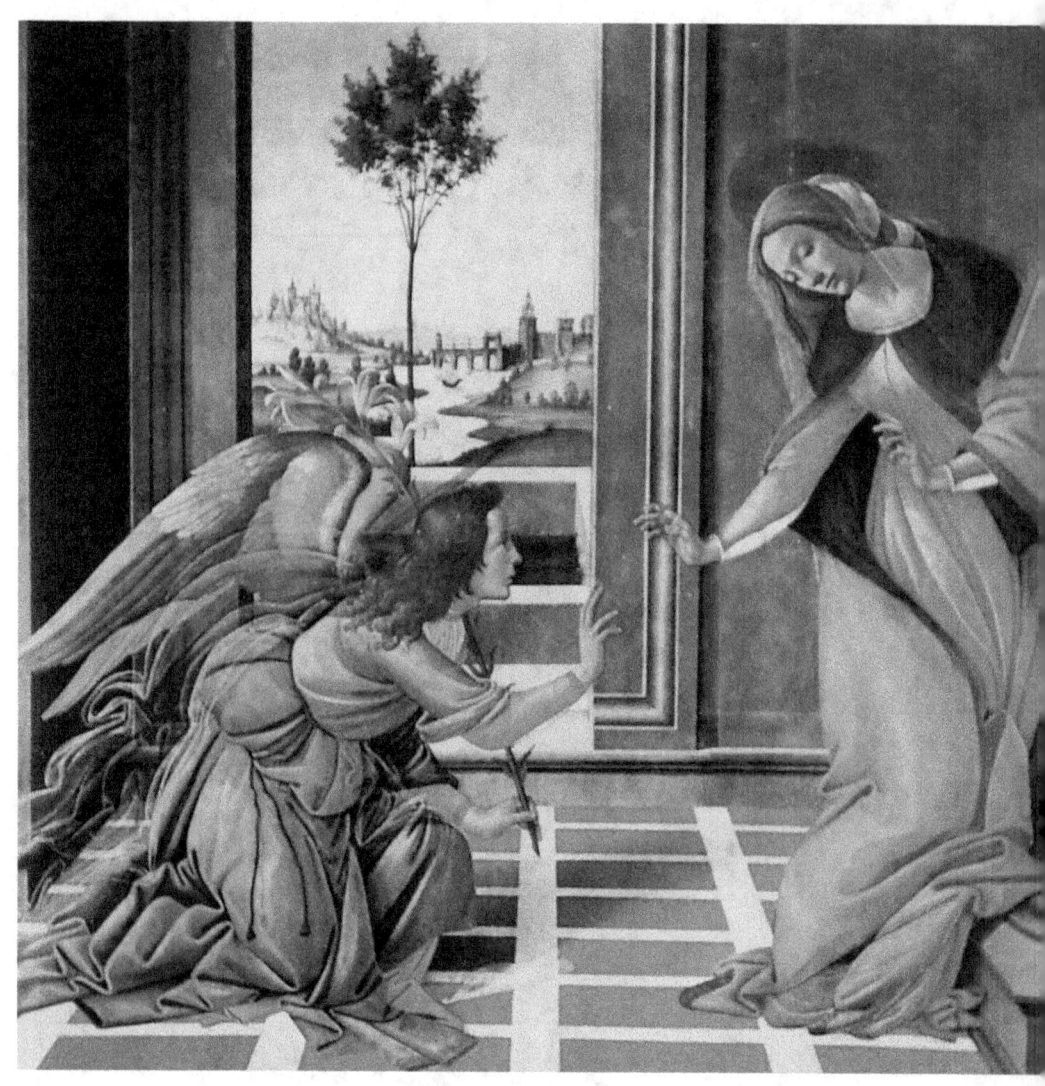

Sandro Botticelli, The Annunciation, Uffizi Gallery, Florence

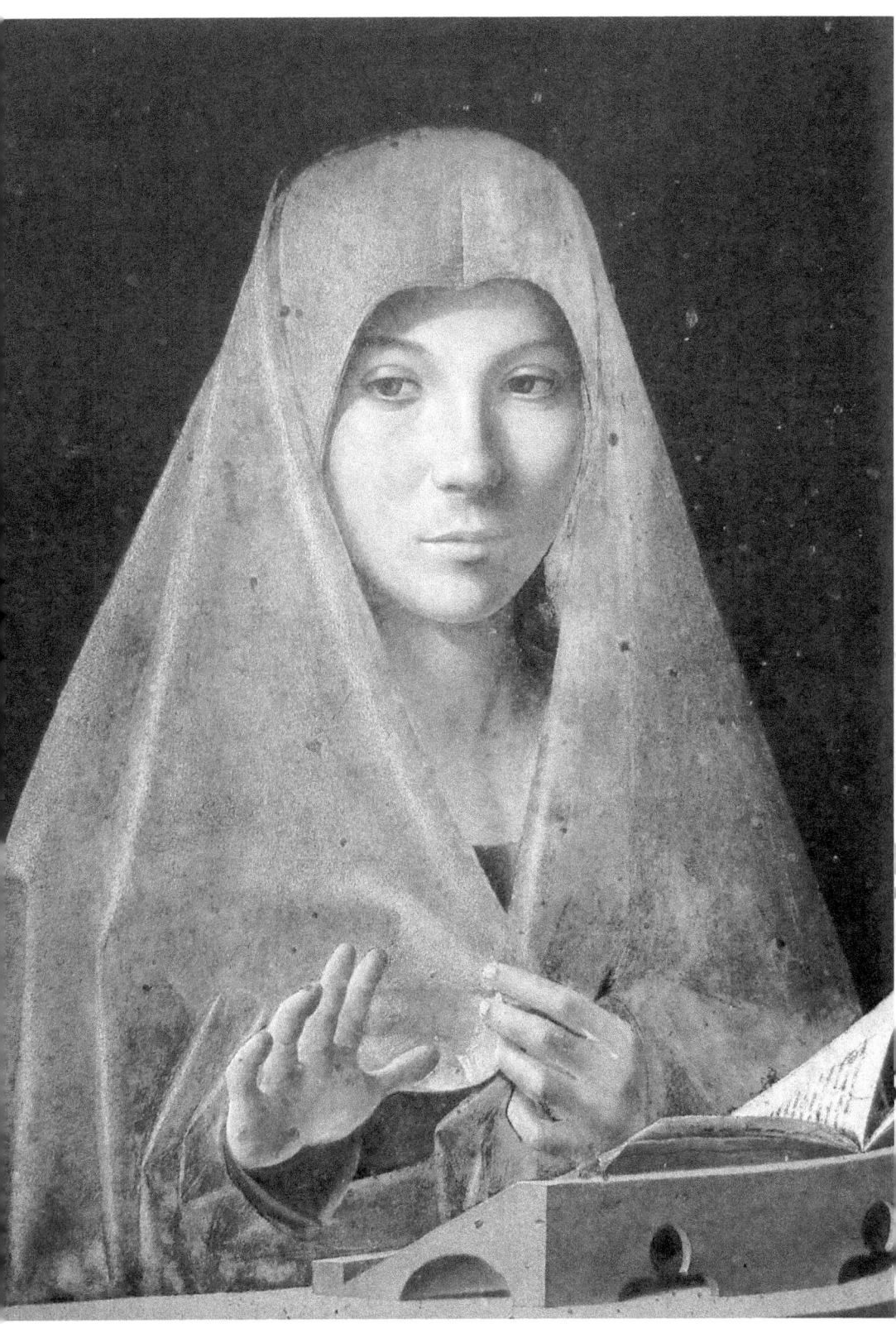

Antonello da Messina, The Virgin of the Annunciation, 1475, Palermo

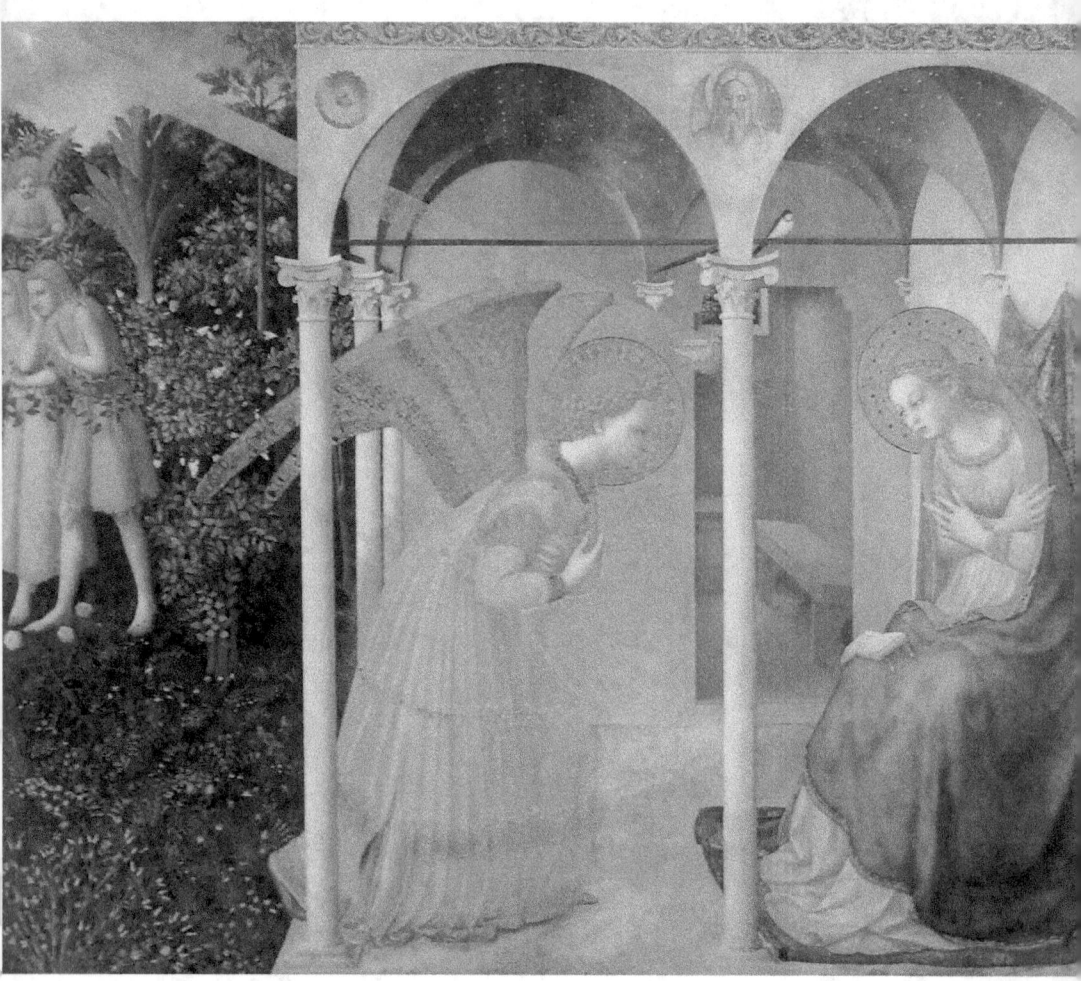

Fra Angelico, Annunciation, Prado, Madrid

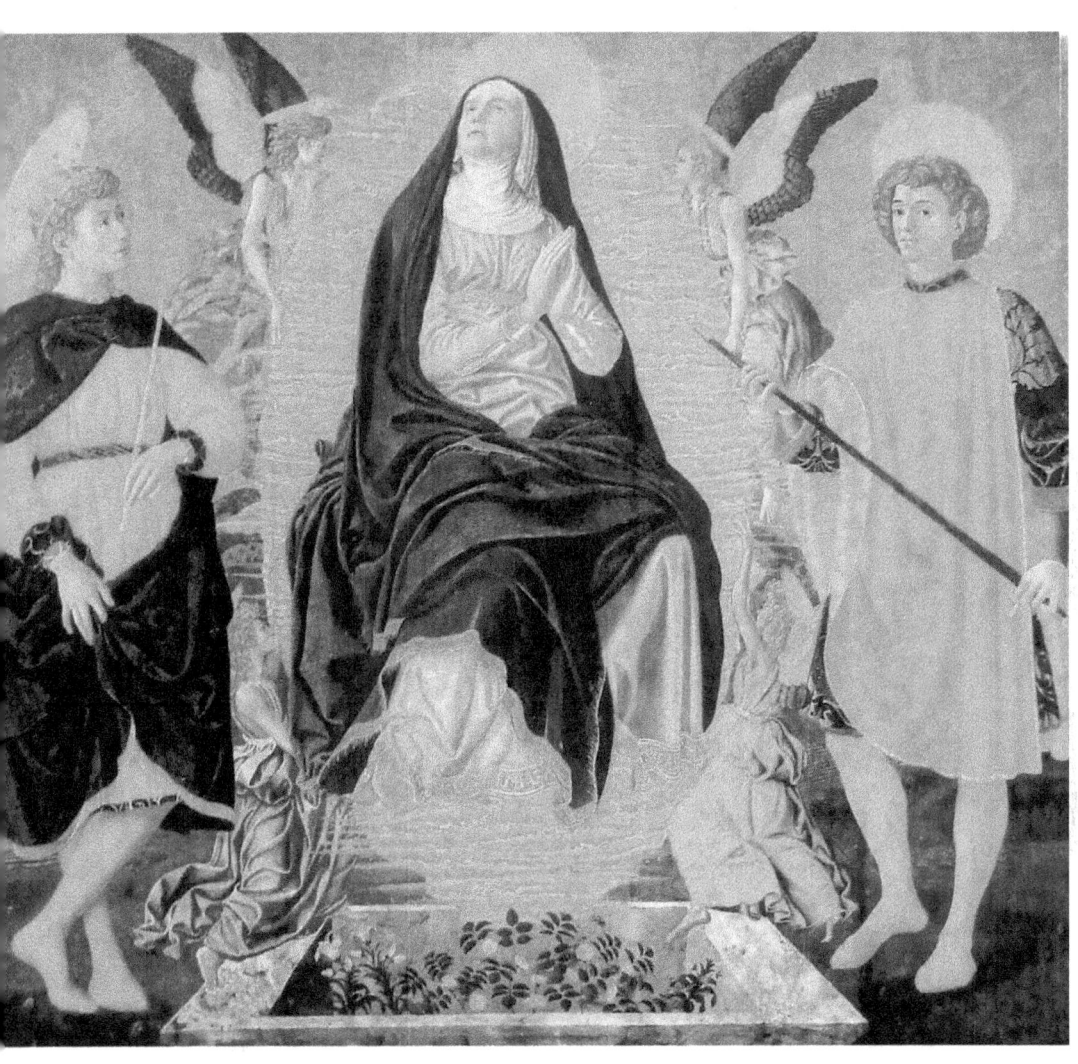

Andrea del Castagno, Assumption, Berlin

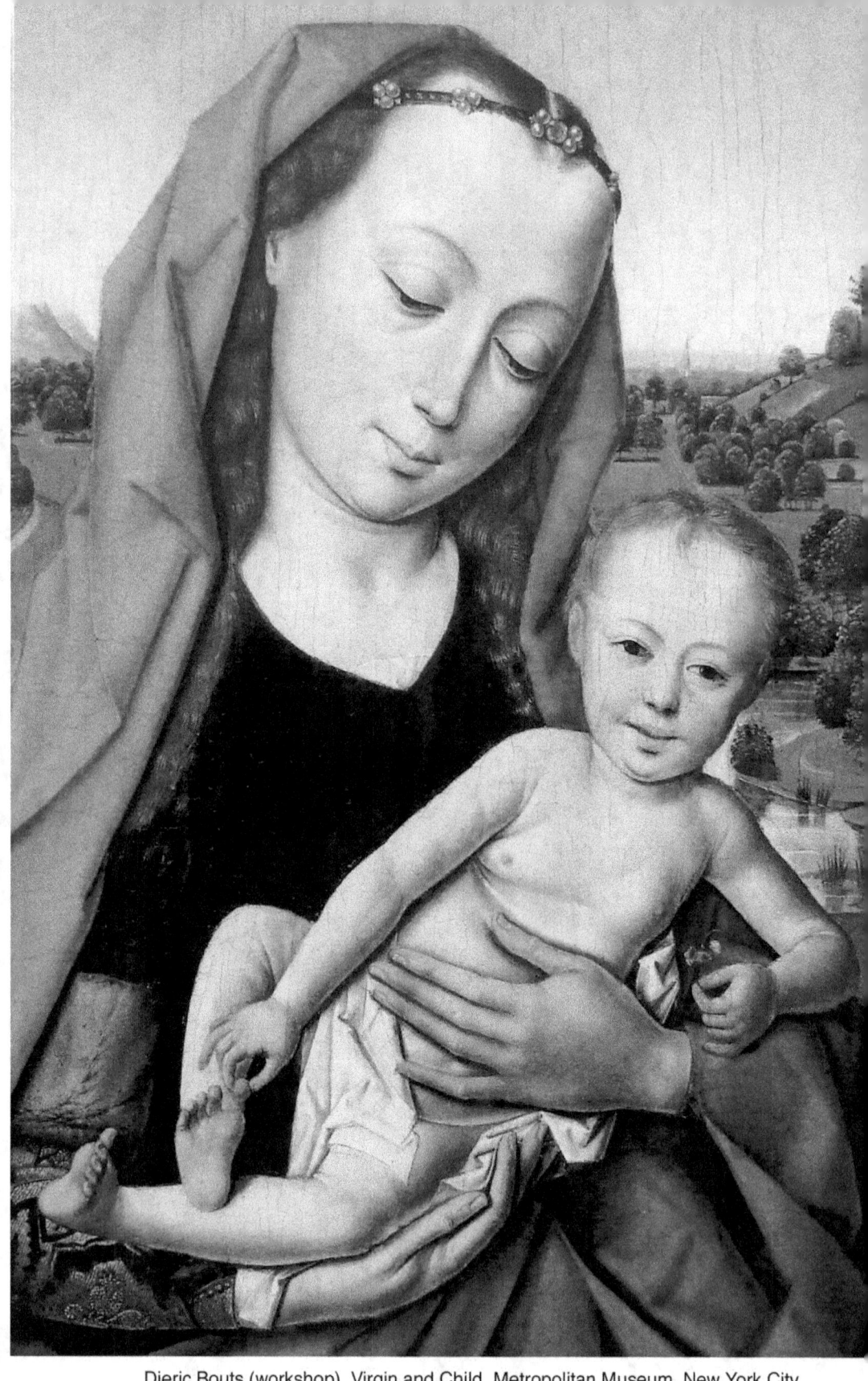

Dieric Bouts (workshop), Virgin and Child, Metropolitan Museum, New York City

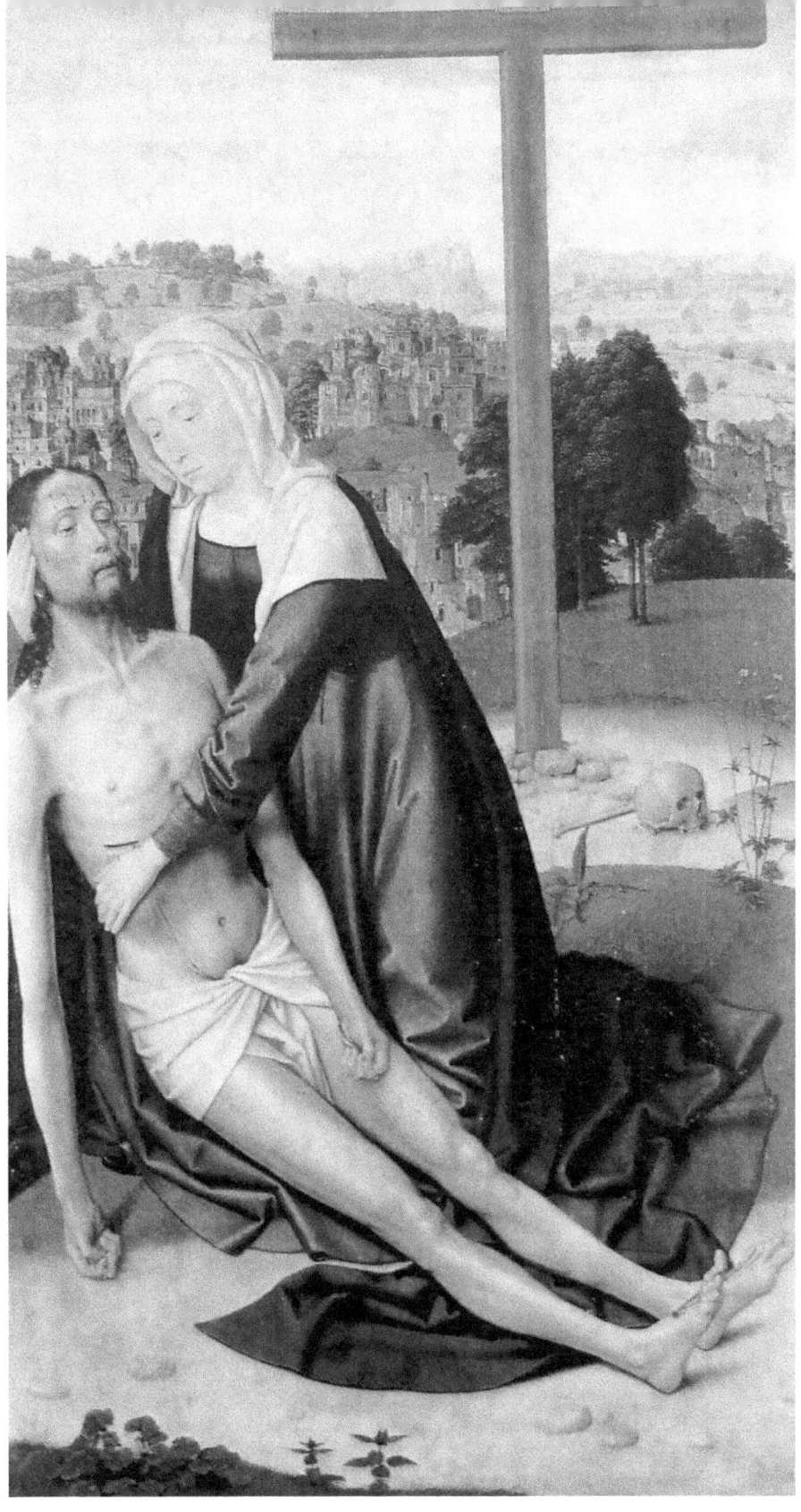

Gerard David, Pietà, Winterhur

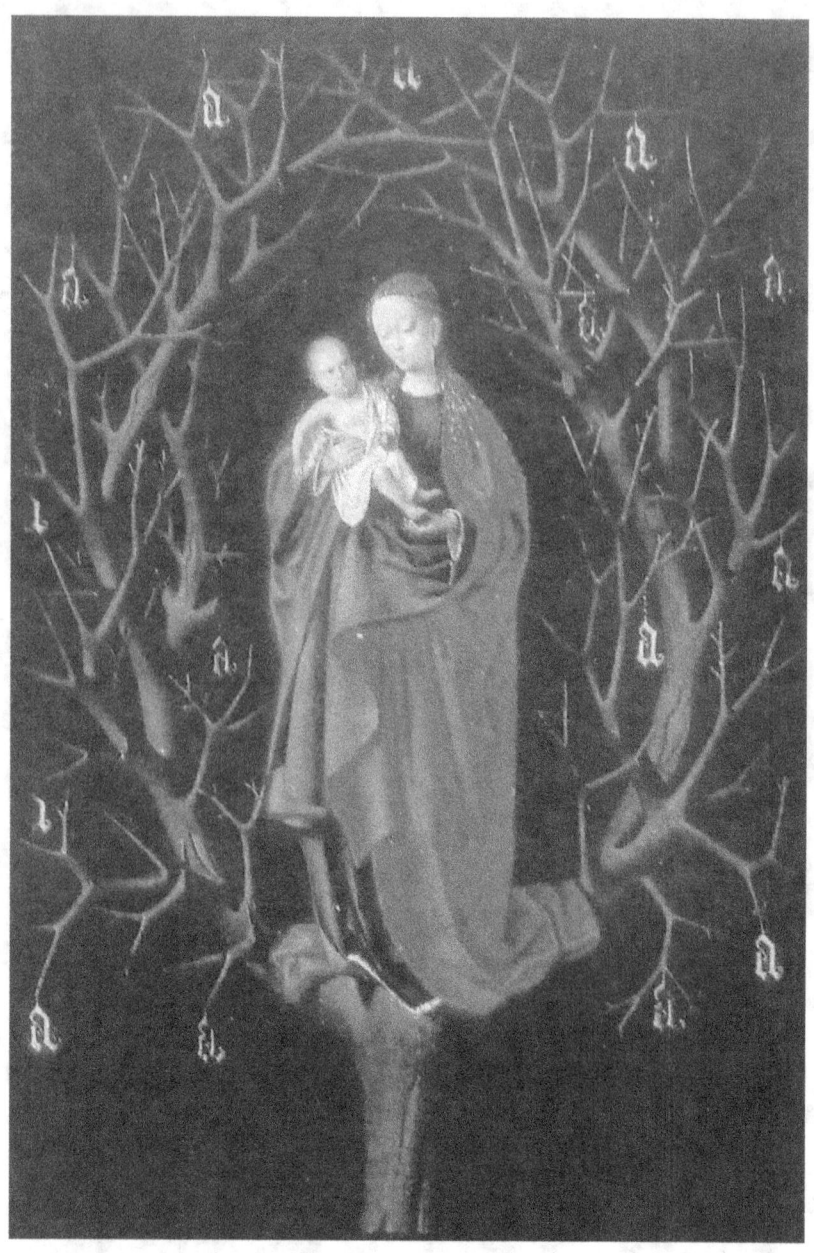

Petrus Christus, Madonna In a Barren Tree, 1450,
Prado, Madrid

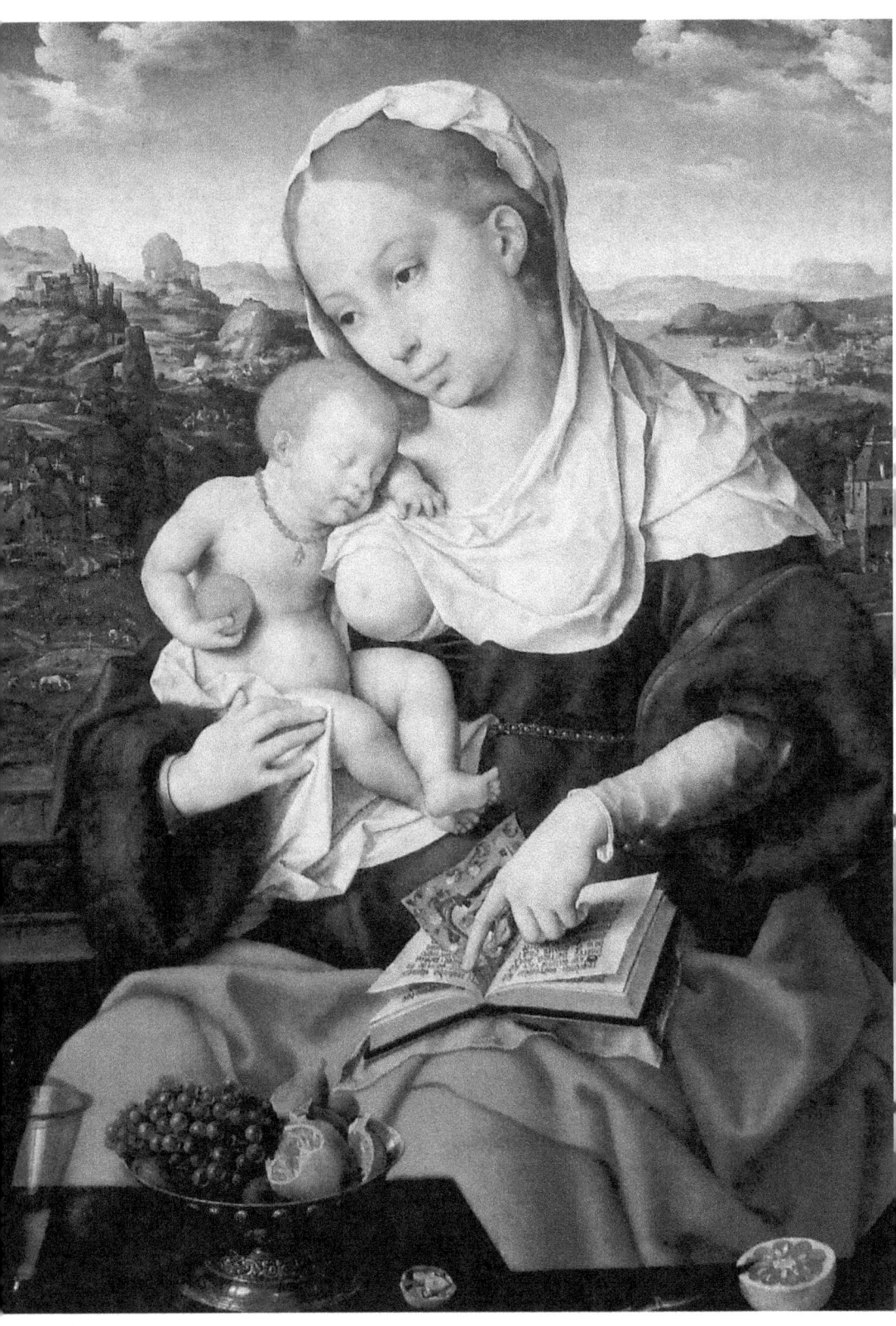

Joos van Cleve, Madonna and Child, Metropolitan Museum,
New York City

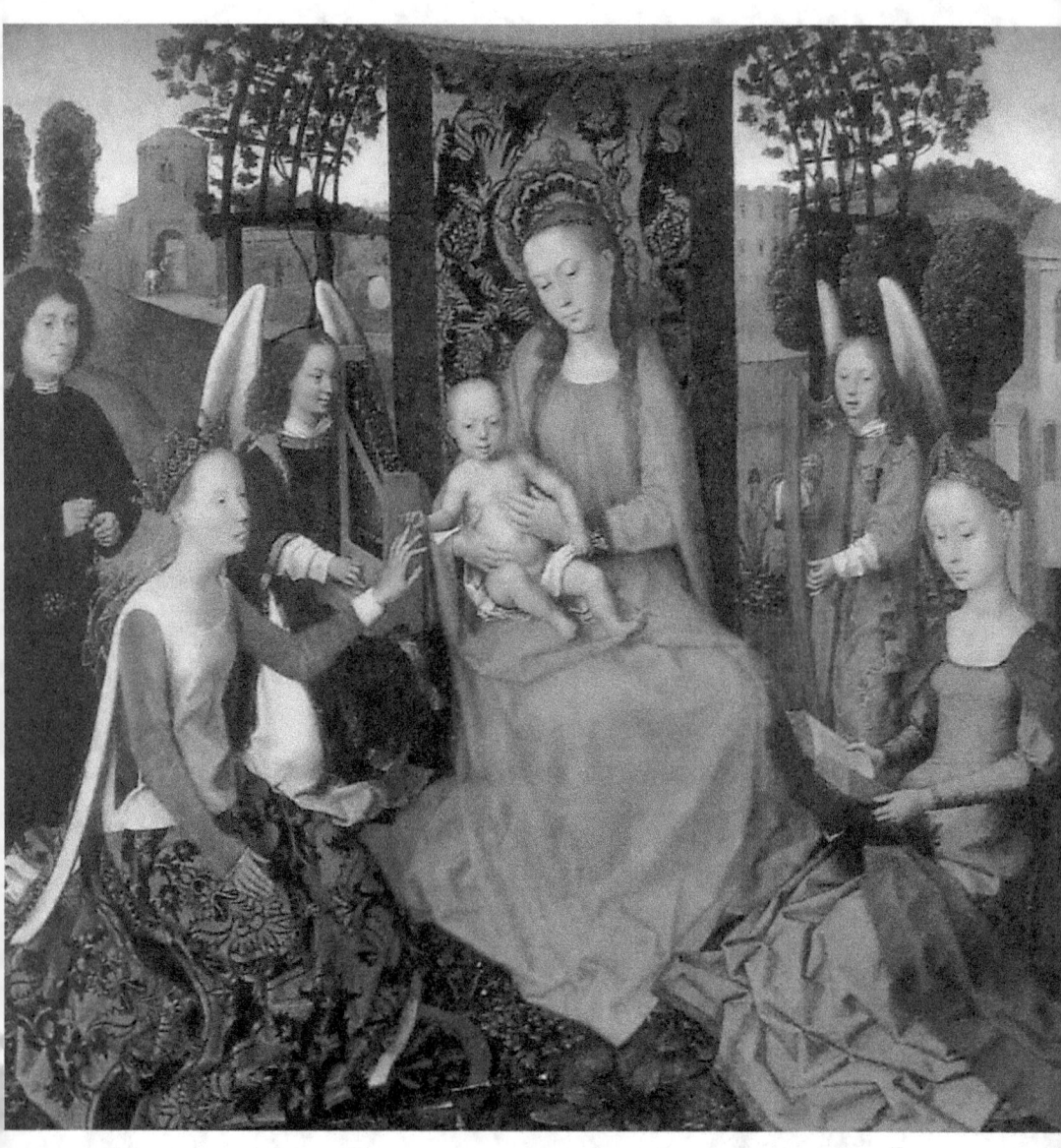

Hans Memling, The Mystic Marriage of St Catherine, Metropolitan
Museum, New York City

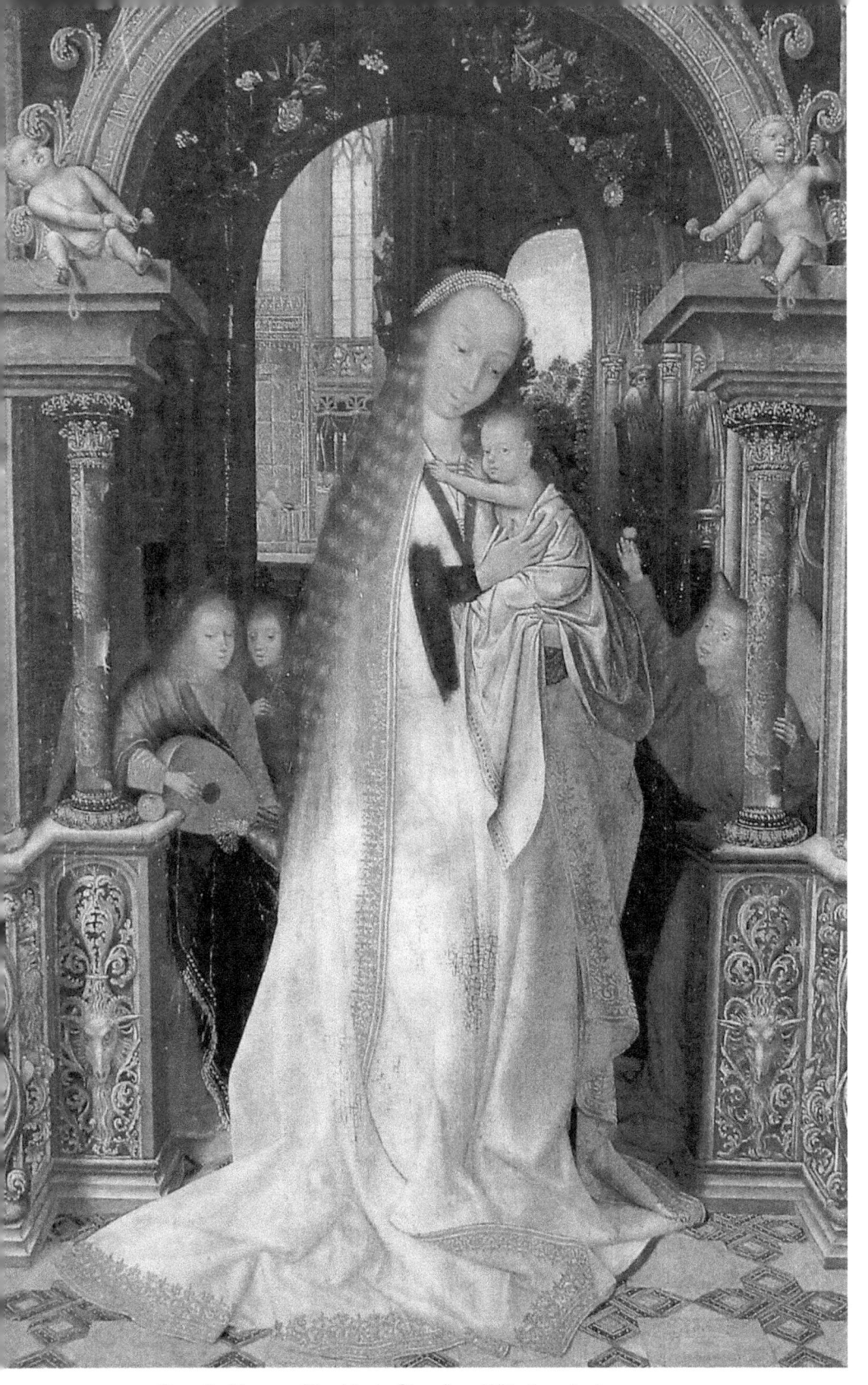

Quentin Massys, The Virgin Standing, With Angels, Lyons

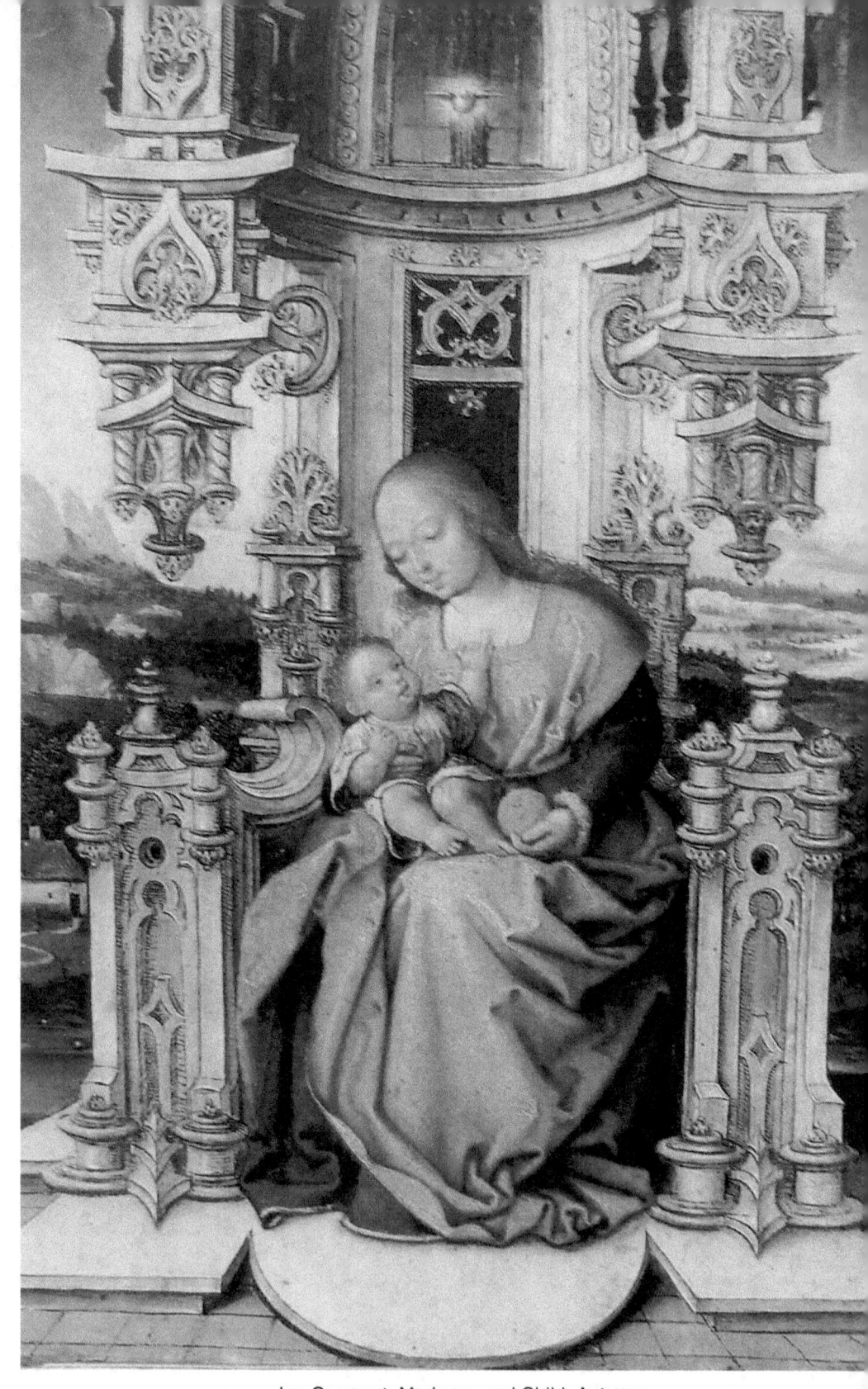

Jan Gossaert, Madonna and Child, Antwerp

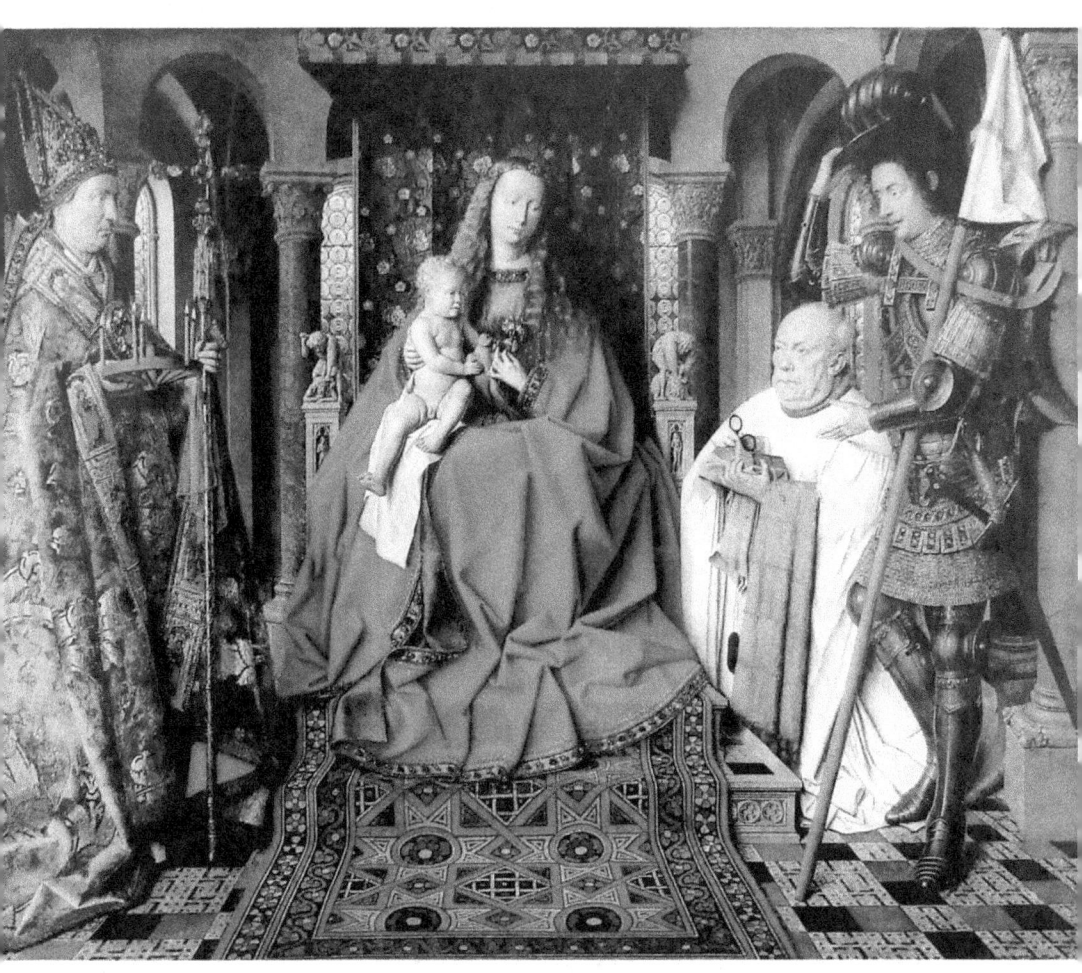

Jan van Eyck, The Paele Madonna, 1436, Bruges

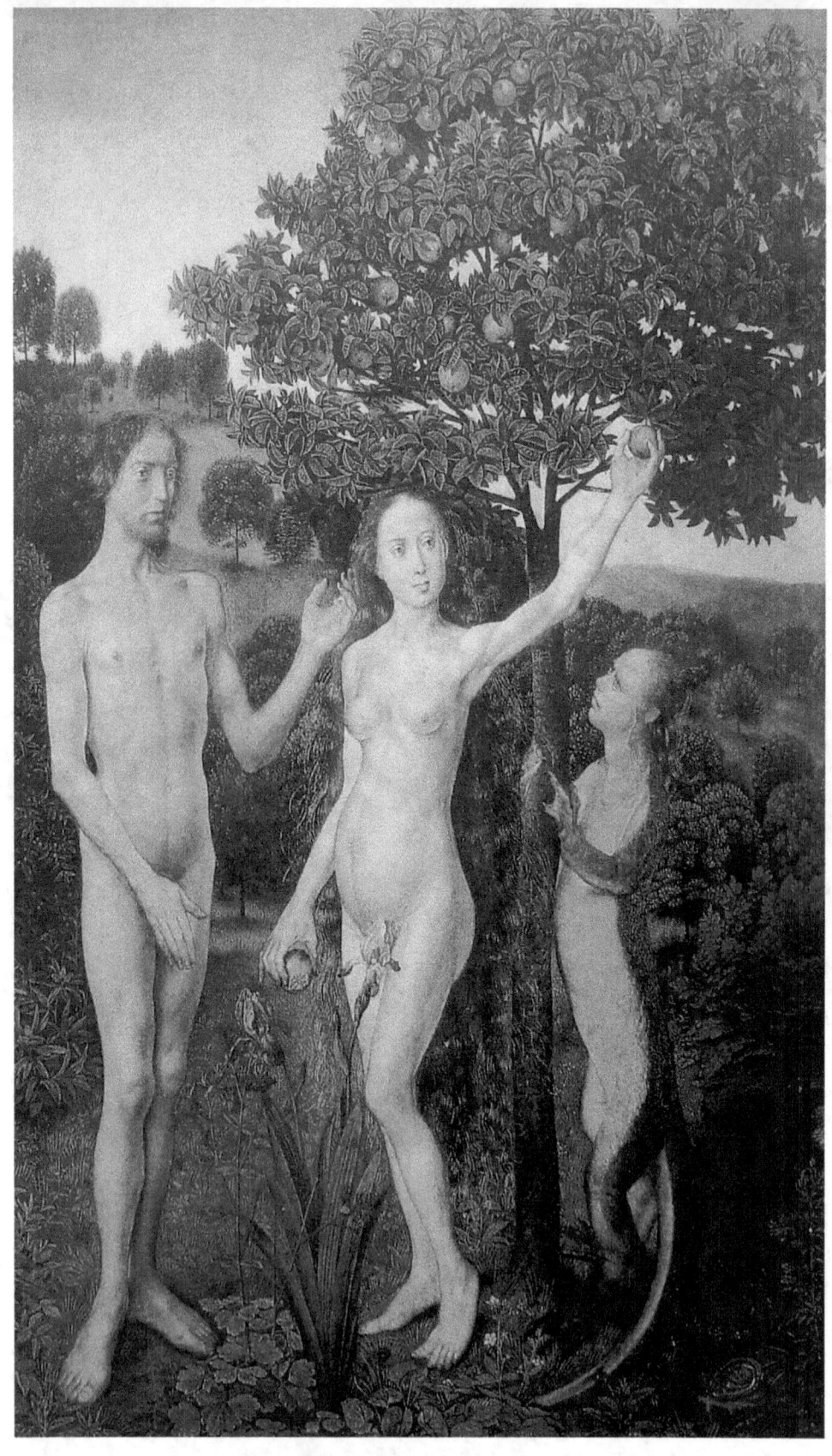

Hugo van der Goes, Fall of Man, 1470, Vienna

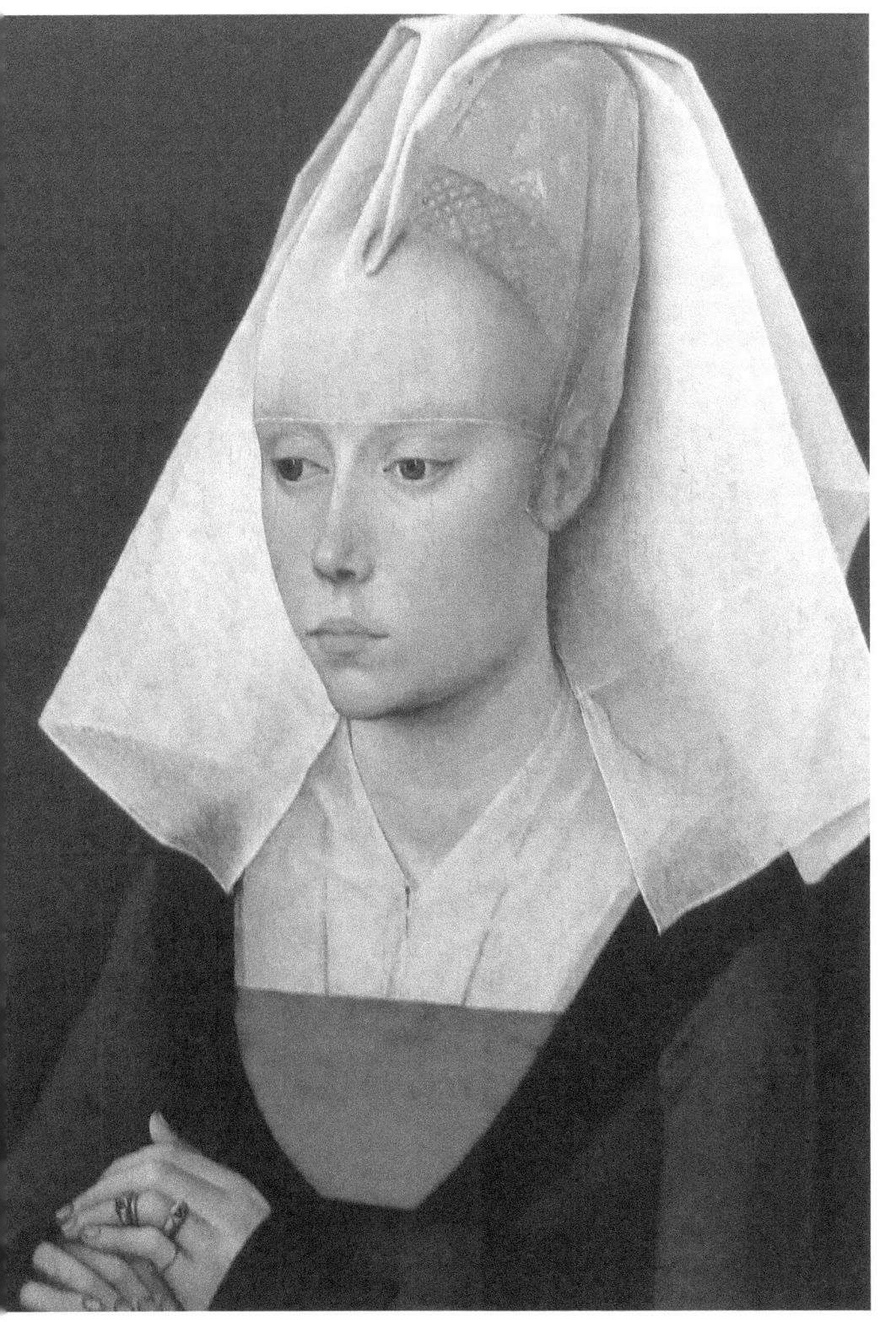

Rogier van der Weyden, Woman Praying, detail, National Gallery, London

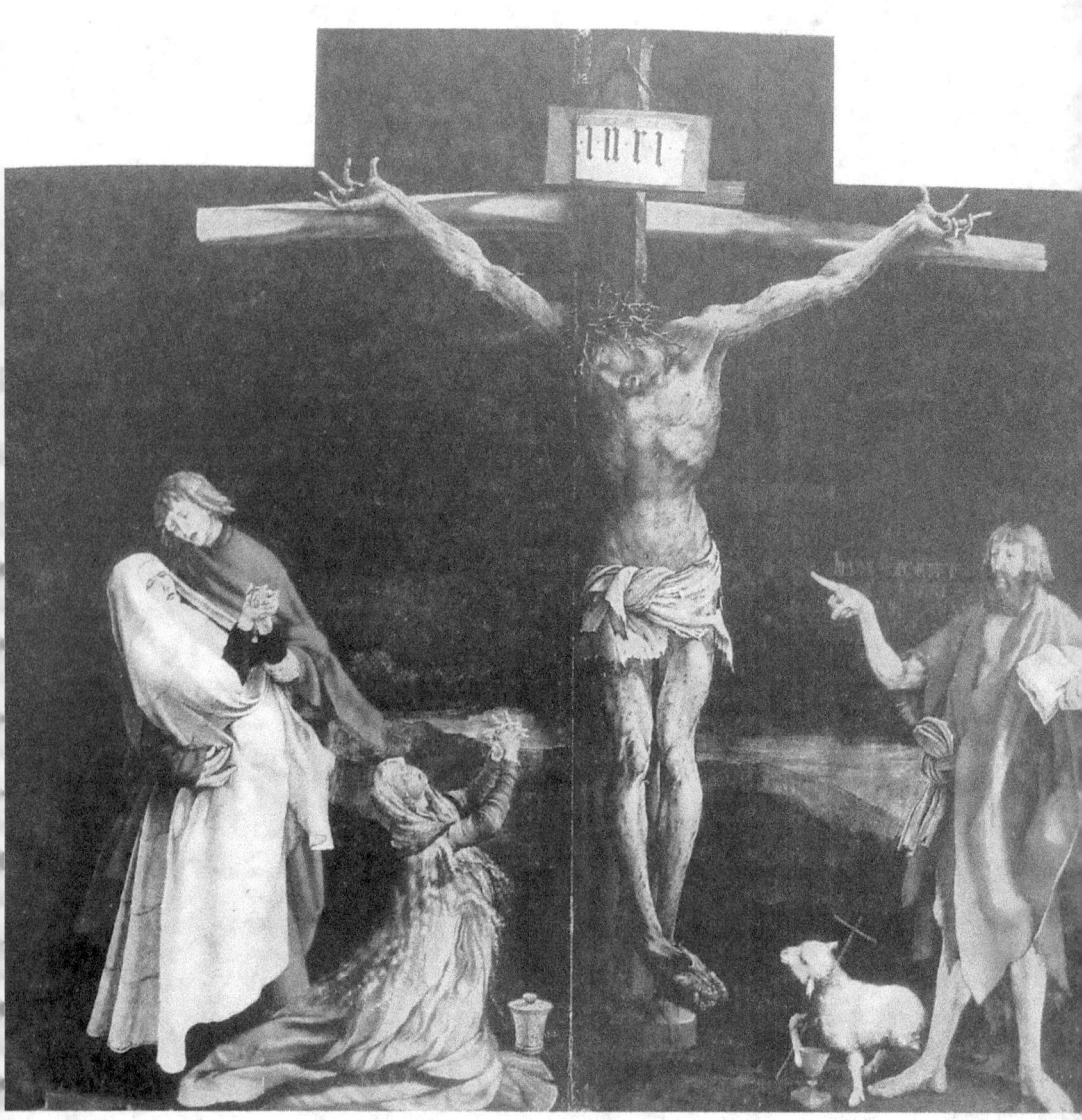

Matthias Grünewald, Crucifixion, Isenheim Altarpiece

MAURICE SENDAK

& the art of children's book illustration

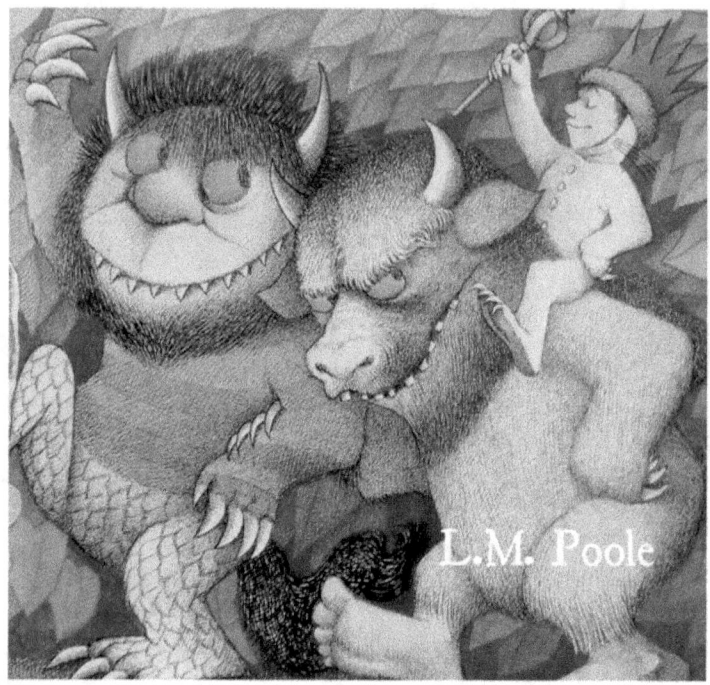

L.M. Poole

Maurice Sendak is the widely acclaimed American children's book author and illustrator. This critical study focuses on his famous trilogy, *Where the Wild Things Are, In the Night Kitchen* and *Outside Over There*, as well as the early works and Sendak's superb depictions of the Grimm Brothers' fairy tales in *The Juniper Tree*. L.M. Poole begins with a chapter on children's book illustration, in particular the treatment of fairy tales. Sendak's work is situated within the history of children's book illustration, and he is compared with many contemporary authors.

Fully illustrated. The book has been revised and updated for this edition.
ISBN 9781861714282 Pbk   ISBN 9781861713469 Hbk

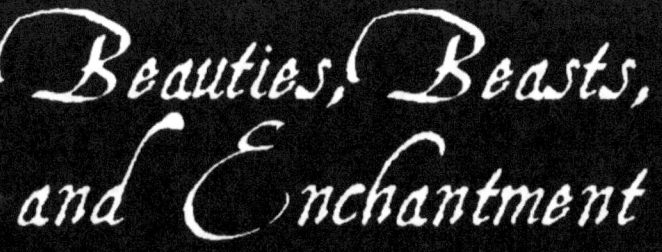

Beauties, Beasts, and Enchantment

CLASSIC FRENCH FAIRY TALES

Translated and with an Introduction
by Jack Zipes

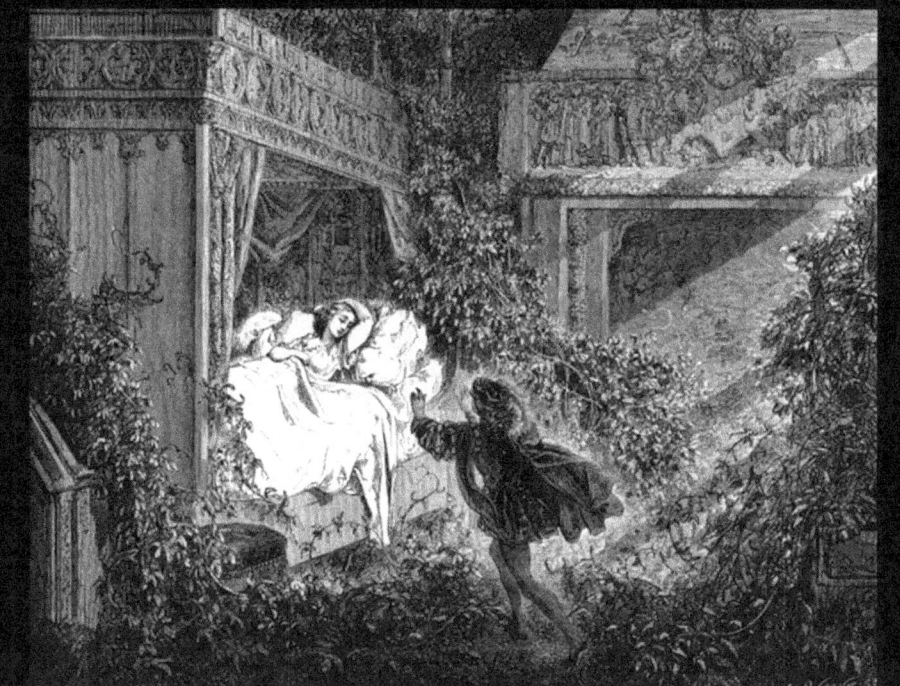

A collection of 36 classic French fairy tales translated by renowned writer Jack Zipes.
Cinderella, Beauty and the Beast, Sleeping Beauty and *Little Red Riding Hood* are among the
classic fairy tales in this amazing book.
Includes illustrations from fairy tale collections.
Jack Zipes has written and published widely on fairy tales.

'Terrific... a succulent array of 17th and 18th century 'salon' fairy tales'
- *The New York Times Book Review*

'These tales are adventurous, thrilling in a way fairy tales are meant to be... The translation
from the French is modern, happily free of archaic and hyperbolic language... a fine and
sophisticated collection' - *New York Tribune*

'Enjoyable to read... a unique collection of French regional folklore' - *Library Journal*

'Charming stories accompanied by attractive pen-and-ink drawings' - *Chattanooga Times*

Introduction and illustrations   612pp.   ISBN 9781861712510 Pbk   ISBN 9781861713193 Hbk

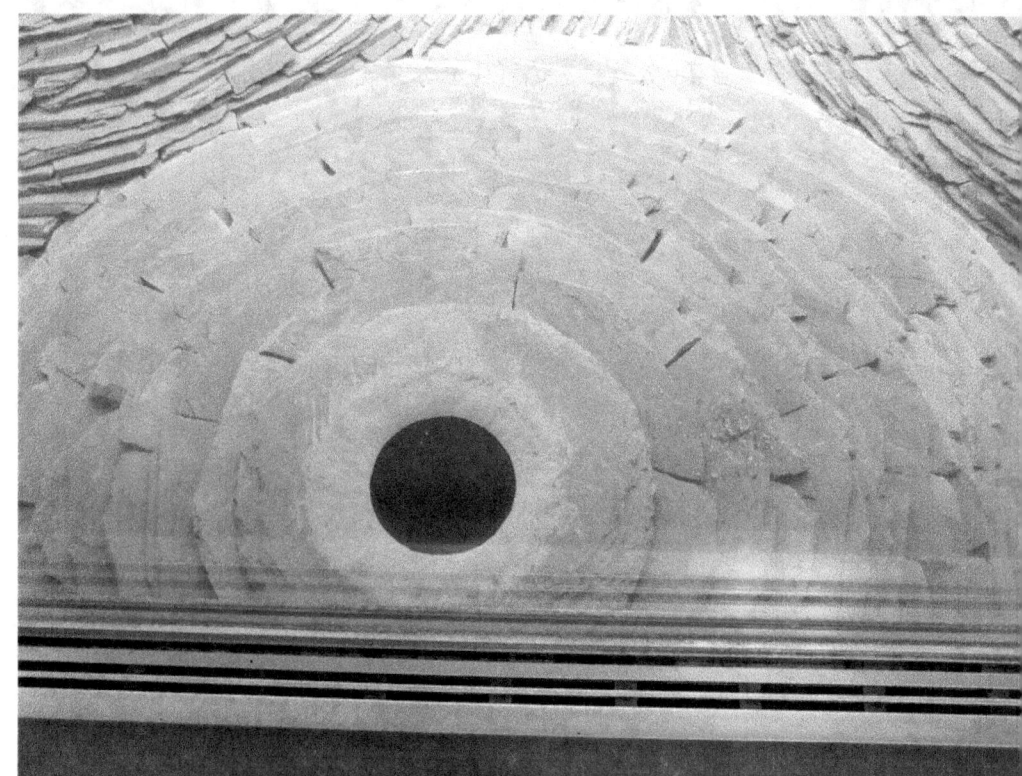

andy goldsworthy
touching nature

WILLIAM MALPAS

Contemporary British sculptor Andy Goldsworthy makes land and
environmental art, a sensitive, intuitive response to nature, light, time,
growth, change, the seasons and the earth. Goldsworthy's sculpture is
becoming ever more popular, appearing in TV documentaries, public works,
and Holocaust memorials. Goldsworthy has exhibited around the world, and
has become one of the foremost contemporary sculptors in Great Britain.

The book has been updated and revised for this new edition.

ISBN 9781861714122 Pbk   ISBN 9781861714138 Hbk
Fully illustrated   www.crmoon.com

CRESCENT MOON PUBLISHING

web: www.crmoon.com e-mail: cresmopub@yahoo.co.uk

ARTS, PAINTING, SCULPTURE

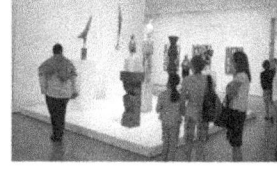

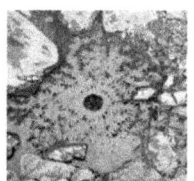

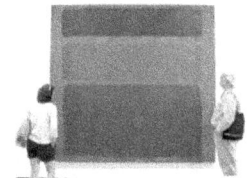

The Art of Andy Goldsworthy
Andy Goldsworthy: Touching Nature
Andy Goldsworthy in Close-Up
Andy Goldsworthy: Pocket Guide
Andy Goldsworthy In America
Land Art: A Complete Guide
The Art of Richard Long
Richard Long: Pocket Guide
Land Art In the UK
Land Art in Close-Up
Land Art In the U.S.A.
Land Art: Pocket Guide
Installation Art in Close-Up
Minimal Art and Artists In the 1960s and After
Colourfield Painting
Land Art DVD, TV documentary
Andy Goldsworthy DVD, TV documentary
The Erotic Object: Sexuality in Sculpture From Prehistory to the Present Day
Sex in Art: Pornography and Pleasure in Painting and Sculpture
Postwar Art
Sacred Gardens: The Garden in Myth, Religion and Art
Glorification: Religious Abstraction in Renaissance and 20th Century Art
Early Netherlandish Painting
Leonardo da Vinci
Piero della Francesca
Giovanni Bellini
Fra Angelico: Art and Religion in the Renaissance
Mark Rothko: The Art of Transcendence
Frank Stella: American Abstract Artist
Jasper Johns
Brice Marden
Alison Wilding: The Embrace of Sculpture
Vincent van Gogh: Visionary Landscapes
Eric Gill: Nuptials of God
Constantin Brancusi: Sculpting the Essence of Things
Max Beckmann
Caravaggio
Gustave Moreau
Egon Schiele: Sex and Death In Purple Stockings
Delizioso Fotografico Fervore: Works In Process 1
Sacro Cuore: Works In Process 2
The Light Eternal: J.M.W. Turner
The Madonna Glorified: Karen Arthurs

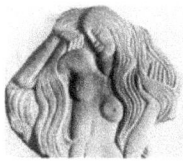

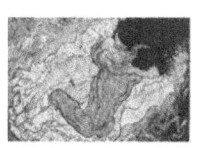

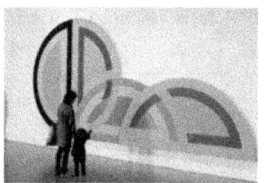

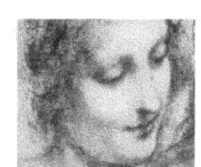

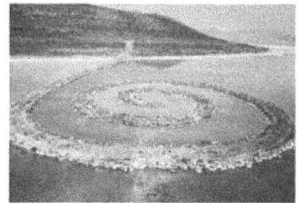

LITERATURE

J.R.R. Tolkien: The Books, The Films, The Whole Cultural Phenomenon
J.R.R. Tolkien: Pocket Guide
Tolkien's Heroic Quest
The *Earthsea* Books of Ursula Le Guin
Beauties, Beasts and Enchantment: Classic French Fairy Tales
German Popular Stories by the Brothers Grimm
Philip Pullman and *His Dark Materials*
Sexing Hardy: Thomas Hardy and Feminism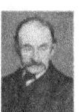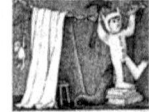
Thomas Hardy's *Tess of the d'Urbervilles*
Thomas Hardy's *Jude the Obscure*
Thomas Hardy: The Tragic Novels
Love and Tragedy: Thomas Hardy
The Poetry of Landscape in Hardy
Wessex Revisited: Thomas Hardy and John Cowper Powys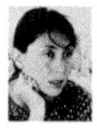
Wolfgang Iser: Essays and Interviews
Petrarch, Dante and the Troubadours
Maurice Sendak and the Art of Children's Book Illustration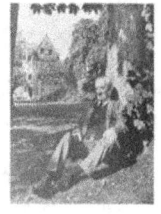
Andrea Dworkin
Cixous, Irigaray, Kristeva: The *Jouissance* of French Feminism
Julia Kristeva: Art, Love, Melancholy, Philosophy, Semiotics and Psychoanalysis
Hélène Cixous I Love You: The *Jouissance* of Writing
Luce Irigaray: Lips, Kissing, and the Politics of Sexual Difference
Peter Redgrove: Here Comes the Flood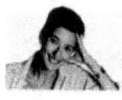
Peter Redgrove: Sex-Magic-Poetry-Cornwall
Lawrence Durrell: Between Love and Death, East and West
Love, Culture & Poetry: Lawrence Durrell
Cavafy: Anatomy of a Soul
German Romantic Poetry: Goethe, Novalis, Heine, Hölderlin
Feminism and Shakespeare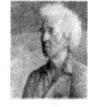
Shakespeare: Love, Poetry & Magic
The Passion of D.H. Lawrence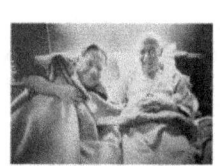
D.H. Lawrence: Symbolic Landscapes
D.H. Lawrence: Infinite Sensual Violence
Rimbaud: Arthur Rimbaud and the Magic of Poetry
The Ecstasies of John Cowper Powys
Sensualism and Mythology: The Wessex Novels of John Cowper Powys
Amorous Life: John Cowper Powys and the Manifestation of Affectivity (H.W. Fawkner)
Postmodern Powys: New Essays on John Cowper Powys (Joe Boulter)
Rethinking Powys: Critical Essays on John Cowper Powys
Paul Bowles & Bernardo Bertolucci
Rainer Maria Rilke
Joseph Conrad: *Heart of Darkness*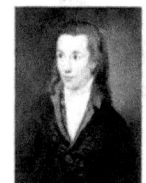
In the Dim Void: Samuel Beckett
Samuel Beckett Goes into the Silence
André Gide: Fiction and Fervour
Jackie Collins and the Blockbuster Novel
Blinded By Her Light: The Love-Poetry of Robert Graves
The Passion of Colours: Travels In Mediterranean Lands
Poetic Forms

POETRY

Ursula Le Guin: Walking In Cornwall
Peter Redgrove: Here Comes The Flood
Peter Redgrove: Sex-Magic-Poetry-Cornwall
Dante: Selections From the Vita Nuova
Petrarch, Dante and the Troubadours
William Shakespeare: Sonnets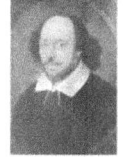
William Shakespeare: Complete Poems
Blinded By Her Light: The Love-Poetry of Robert Graves
Emily Dickinson: Selected Poems
Emily Brontë: Poems
Thomas Hardy: Selected Poems
Percy Bysshe Shelley: Poems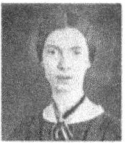
John Keats: Selected Poems
Joh n Keats: Poems of 1820
D.H. Lawrence: Selected Poems
Edmund Spenser: Poems
Edmund Spenser: Amoretti
John Donne: Poems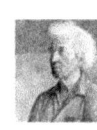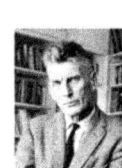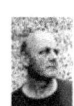
Henry Vaughan: Poems
Sir Thomas Wyatt: Poems
Robert Herrick: Selected Poems
Rilke: Space, Essence and Angels in the Poetry of Rainer Maria Rilke
Rainer Maria Rilke: Selected Poems
Friedrich Hölderlin: Selected Poems
Arseny Tarkovsky: Selected Poems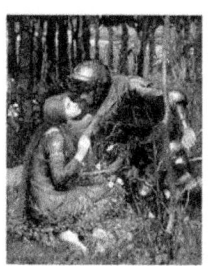
Arthur Rimbaud: Selected Poems
Arthur Rimbaud: A Season in Hell
Arthur Rimbaud and the Magic of Poetry
Novalis: Hymns To the Night
German Romantic Poetry
Paul Verlaine: Selected Poems
Elizaethan Sonnet Cycles
D.J. Enright: By-Blows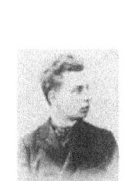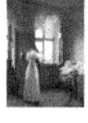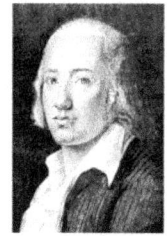
Jeremy Reed: Brigitte's Blue Heart
Jeremy Reed: Claudia Schiffer's Red Shoes
Gorgeous Little Orpheus
Radiance: New Poems
Crescent Moon Book of Nature Poetry
Crescent Moon Book of Love Poetry
Crescent Moon Book of Mystical Poetry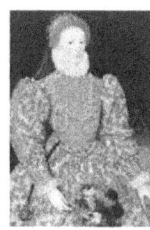
Crescent Moon Book of Elizabethan Love Poetry
Crescent Moon Book of Metaphysical Poetry
Crescent Moon Book of Romantic Poetry
Pagan America: New American Poetry

MEDIA, CINEMA, FEMINISM and CULTURAL STUDIES

J.R.R. Tolkien: The Books, The Films, The Whole Cultural Phenomenon
J.R.R. Tolkien: Pocket Guide
The *Lord of the Rings* Movies: Pocket Guide
The Cinema of Hayao Miyazaki
Hayao Miyazaki: *Princess Mononoke*: Pocket Movie Guide
Hayao Miyazaki: *Spirited Away*: Pocket Movie Guide
Tim Burton : Hallowe'en For Hollywood
Ken Russell

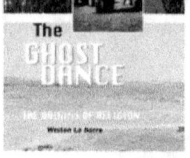

Ken Russell: *Tommy*: Pocket Movie Guide
The Ghost Dance: The Origins of Religion
The Peyote Cult
Cixous, Irigaray, Kristeva: The *Jouissance* of French Feminism
Julia Kristeva: Art, Love, Melancholy, Philosophy, Semiotics and Psychoanalysis
Luce Irigaray: Lips, Kissing, and the Politics of Sexual Difference
Hélène Cixous I Love You: The *Jouissance* of Writing
Andrea Dworkin

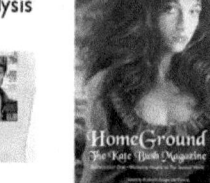

'Cosmo Woman': The World of Women's Magazines
Women in Pop Music
HomeGround: The Kate Bush Anthology
Discovering the Goddess (Geoffrey Ashe)
The Poetry of Cinema

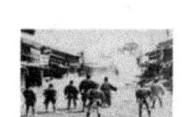

The Sacred Cinema of Andrei Tarkovsky
Andrei Tarkovsky: Pocket Guide
Andrei Tarkovsky: *Mirror*: Pocket Movie Guide

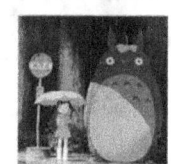

Andrei Tarkovsky: *The Sacrifice*: Pocket Movie Guide
Walerian Borowczyk: Cinema of Erotic Dreams
Jean-Luc Godard: The Passion of Cinema

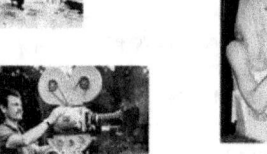

Jean-Luc Godard: *Hail Mary*: Pocket Movie Guide
Jean-Luc Godard: *Contempt*: Pocket Movie Guide
Jean-Luc Godard: *Pierrot le Fou*: Pocket Movie Guide
John Hughes and Eighties Cinema
Ferris Bueller's Day Off: Pocket Movie Guide

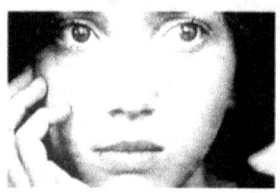

Jean-Luc Godard: Pocket Guide
The Cinema of Richard Linklater
Liv Tyler: Star In Ascendance
Blade Runner and the Films of Philip K. Dick
Paul Bowles and Bernardo Bertolucci
Media Hell: Radio, TV and the Press
An Open Letter to the BBC
Detonation Britain: Nuclear War in the UK
Feminism and Shakespeare
Wild Zones: Pornography, Art and Feminism
Sex in Art: Pornography and Pleasure in Painting and Sculpture
Sexing Hardy: Thomas Hardy and Feminism

The Light Eternal is a model monograph, an exemplary job. The subject matter of the book is beautifully
organised and dead on beam. (Lawrence Durrell)
It is amazing for me to see my work treated with such passion and respect. (Andrea Dworkin)

CRESCENT MOON PUBLISHING
P.O. Box 1312, Maidstone, Kent, ME14 5XU, Great Britain. www.crmoon.com

cresmopub@yahoo.co.uk   www.crescentmoon.org.uk